God ♥s you!

Presented to

....

From

....

On this date

....

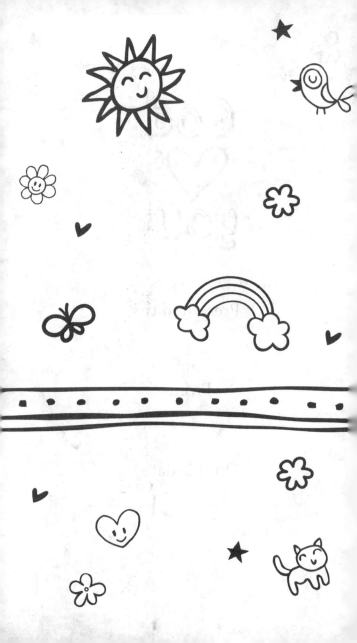

God ♥s me

A Bible Promise Book for Girls

BARBOUR
PUBLISHING

© 2013 by Barbour Publishing, Inc.

Written and compiled by Brigitta Nortker.

Print ISBN 978-1-62416-137-7

eBook Editions:
Adobe Digital Edition (.epub) 978-1-62416-395-1
Kindle and MobiPocket Edition (.prc) 978-1-62416-394-4

Published by Barbour Publishing, Inc., P.O. Box 719, Uhrichsville, Ohio 44683, www.barbourbooks.com

Our mission is to publish and distribute inspirational products offering exceptional value and biblical encouragement to the masses.

Member of the
Evangelical Christian
Publishers Association

Printed in the United States of America.
The Maple Press Co., York, PA 17406; June 2013; D10003942

Contents

Introduction

The world is full of conflicting messages on life's most important issues. What does it mean to truly forgive? Does God really think I'm beautiful? Is it possible to have joy even during hard times? Does God always listen when I pray? And does He have a plan for my life?

In His loving-kindness, God has answered all of these questions—and many more—in His Word, the Bible. Whatever is on your mind...whatever you need...you can *always* find answers and direction for your life in scripture.

This collection of Bible verses is an easy-to-use reference when you need answers about life. In these pages, you'll find carefully selected verses that address topics like comfort, strength, hope, God's promises, joy, prayer, and understanding—a wonderful way to refresh your heart with regular reminders of God's love for you!

God
Comforts
Me

Dear God, sometimes I get overwhelmed and discouraged when I go through a hard time in my life. I find comfort in knowing that You are always with me, guiding me, soothing me, and encouraging me. Help me to remember that You are the one I should turn to for comfort. Others come and go, but Your love and support never waver and will never be separated from me. Amen.

Christ encourages you, and his love comforts you. God's Spirit unites you, and you are concerned for others.

PHILIPPIANS 2:1 CEV

Even though I walk through the darkest valley, I will fear no evil, for you are with me; your rod and your staff, they comfort me.

PSALM 23:4 NIV

Remember your promise to me; it is my only hope. Your promise revives me; it comforts me in all my troubles.

PSALM 119:49–50 NLT

May our Lord Jesus Christ himself and God our Father encourage you and strengthen you in every good thing you do and say. God loved us, and through his grace he gave us a good hope and encouragement that continues forever.

2 THESSALONIANS 2:16–17 NCV

Nevertheless God, who comforts the downcast, comforted us.

2 CORINTHIANS 7:6 NKJV

Show me a sign for good, that those who hate me may see it and be ashamed, because You, LORD, have helped me and comforted me.

PSALM 86:17 NKJV

Heavens and earth, be happy. Mountains, shout with joy, because the LORD comforts his people and will have pity on those who suffer.

ISAIAH 49:13 NCV

I find true comfort, LORD, because your laws have stood the test of time.

PSALM 119:52 CEV

Praise be to the God and Father of our Lord Jesus Christ, the Father of compassion and the God of all comfort, who comforts us in all our troubles, so that we can comfort those in any trouble with the comfort we ourselves receive from God. For just as we share abundantly in the sufferings of Christ, so also our comfort abounds through Christ.

2 CORINTHIANS 1:3–5 NIV

Though you have made me see troubles, many and bitter, you will restore my life again; from the depths of the earth you will again bring me up. You will increase my honor and comfort me once more.

PSALM 71:20–21 NIV

But now you should forgive him and comfort him to keep him from having too much sadness and giving up completely.

2 CORINTHIANS 2:7 NCV

And I will pray the Father, and he shall give you another Comforter, that he may abide with you for ever.

JOHN 14:16 KJV

Teach them to do everything I have told you. I will be with you always, even until the end of the world.

MATTHEW 28:20 CEV

He will swallow up death forever. The Sovereign LORD will wipe away the tears from all faces; he will remove his people's disgrace from all the earth.

ISAIAH 25:8 NIV

I serve you, LORD. Comfort me with your love, just as you have promised.

PSALM 119:76 CEV

"God blesses those who mourn, for they will be comforted."

MATTHEW 5:4 NLT

Come near to God, and God will come near to you. You sinners, clean sin out of your lives. You who are trying to follow God and the world at the same time, make your thinking pure.

JAMES 4:8 NCV

Finally, brethren, farewell. Become complete. Be of good comfort, be of one mind, live in peace; and the God of love and peace will be with you.

2 CORINTHIANS 13:11 NKJV

If you are tired from carrying heavy burdens, come to me and I will give you rest.

MATTHEW 11:28 CEV

"As a mother comforts her child, so I'll comfort you. You will be comforted."

ISAIAH 66:13 MSG

For I am convinced that neither death nor life, neither angels nor demons, neither the present nor the future, nor any powers, neither height nor depth, nor anything else in all creation, will be able to separate us from the love of God that is in Christ Jesus our Lord.

ROMANS 8:38–40 NIV

This is my comfort and consolation in my affliction: that Your word has revived me and given me life.

PSALM 119:50 AMP

"I will praise you, LORD. Although you were angry with me, your anger has turned away and you have comforted me."

ISAIAH 12:1 NIV

"I will turn their mourning into gladness; I will give them comfort and joy instead of sorrow."

JEREMIAH 31:13 NIV

We suffer in the hope that you will be comforted and saved. And because we are comforted, you will also be comforted, as you patiently endure suffering like ours. You never disappoint us. You suffered as much as we did, and we know that you will be comforted as we were.

2 CORINTHIANS 1:6–7 CEV

And now, dear children, continue in him, so that when he appears we may be confident and unashamed before him at his coming.

1 JOHN 2:28 NIV

"May the LORD bless you and keep you. May the LORD show you his kindness and have mercy on you. May the LORD watch over you and give you peace."

NUMBERS 6:24–26 NCV

For you know that we dealt with each of you as a father deals with his own children, encouraging, comforting and urging you to live lives worthy of God, who calls you into his kingdom and glory.

1 THESSALONIANS 2:11–12 NIV

"I have seen their ways, but I will heal them; I will guide them and restore comfort."

ISAIAH 57:18 NIV

But you, dear friends, must build each other up in your most holy faith, pray in the power of the Holy Spirit, and await the mercy of our Lord Jesus Christ, who will bring you eternal life. In this way, you will keep yourselves safe in God's love.

JUDE 1:20–21 NLT

Anyone who meets a testing challenge head-on and manages to stick it out is mighty fortunate. For such persons loyally in love with God, the reward is life and more life.

JAMES 1:12 MSG

For the Spirit God gave us does not make us timid, but gives us power, love and self-discipline.

2 TIMOTHY 1:7 NIV

God is our refuge and strength, always ready to help in times of trouble. So we will not fear when earthquakes come and the mountains crumble into the sea.

PSALM 46:1–2 NLT

The LORD God is waiting to show how kind he is and to have pity on you. The LORD always does right; he blesses those who trust him.

ISAIAH 30:18 CEV

I pray that from his glorious, unlimited resources he will empower you with inner strength through his Spirit. Then Christ will make his home in your hearts as you trust in him. Your roots will grow down into God's love and keep you strong. And may you have the power to understand, as all God's people should, how wide, how long, how high, and how deep his love is.

EPHESIANS 3:16–18 NLT

"I am the LORD, and I do not change."

MALACHI 3:6 NLT

Whoever dwells in the shelter of the Most High will rest in the shadow of the Almighty.

PSALM 91:1 NIV

My flesh and my heart may fail, but God is the strength of my heart and my portion forever.

PSALM 73:26 NIV

He will help the poor when they cry out and will save the needy when no one else will help. He will be kind to the weak and poor, and he will save their lives. He will save them from cruel people who try to hurt them, because their lives are precious to him.

PSALM 72:12–14 NCV

"Blessed is the man who trusts in the LORD, and whose hope is the LORD."

JEREMIAH 17:7 NKJV

I know what you are like! But I will heal you, lead you, and give you comfort, until those who are mourning start singing my praises. No matter where you are, I, the LORD, will heal you and give you peace.

ISAIAH 57:18–19 CEV

God
Forgives
Me

Heavenly Father, it's hard
to believe that no matter what
I do, You will always forgive me.
You have not only forgiven all
of my sins—past and present—
but You will continue to forgive
my sins in the future and extend
me grace, as long as I ask.
You are the perfect example
of goodness and mercy.
When others hurt my feelings
or offend me, remind me of
Your grace and help me to
forgive and move on, even
when I don't feel like it. Amen.

"You are a forgiving God, gracious and compassionate, slow to anger and abounding in love."

NEHEMIAH 9:17 NIV

"Then if my people, who are called by my name, will humble themselves, if they will pray and seek me and stop their evil ways, I will hear them from heaven. I will forgive their sin, and I will heal their land."

2 CHRONICLES 7:14 NCV

Blessed is the one whose transgressions are forgiven, whose sins are covered.

PSALM 32:1 NIV

Bless the LORD, O my soul, and forget not all His benefits: who forgives all your iniquities, who heals all your diseases, who redeems your life from destruction, who crowns you with lovingkindness and tender mercies.

PSALM 103:2–4 NKJV

If we confess our sins, he is faithful and just and will forgive us our sins and purify us from all unrighteousness.

1 JOHN 1:9 NIV

"For if you forgive other people when they sin against you, your heavenly Father will also forgive you. But if you do not forgive others their sins, your Father will not forgive your sins."

MATTHEW 6:14–15 NIV

And be ye kind one to another, tenderhearted, forgiving one another, even as God for Christ's sake hath forgiven you.

EPHESIANS 4:32 KJV

Then Peter came to him and asked, "Lord, how often should I forgive someone who sins against me? Seven times?" "No, not seven times," Jesus replied, "but seventy times seven!"

MATTHEW 18:21–22 NLT

Whenever you stand up to pray, you must forgive what others have done to you. Then your Father in heaven will forgive your sins.

MARK 11:25 CEV

"Take heed to yourselves. If your brother sins against you, rebuke him; and if he repents, forgive him. And if he sins against you seven times in a day, and seven times in a day returns to you, saying, 'I repent,' you shall forgive him."

LUKE 17:3–4 NKJV

When people sin, you should forgive and comfort them, so they won't give up in despair. You should make them sure of your love for them.

2 CORINTHIANS 2:7–8 CEV

Who is a God like you, who pardons sin and forgives the transgression of the remnant of his inheritance? You do not stay angry forever but delight to show mercy. You will again have compassion on us; you will tread our sins underfoot and hurl all our iniquities into the depths of the sea.

MICAH 7:18–19 NIV

Forgive anyone who offends you. Remember, the Lord forgave you, so you must forgive others.

COLOSSIANS 3:13 NLT

So turn to God! Give up your sins, and you will be forgiven.

ACTS 3:19 CEV

He saved us, not because of the righteous things we had done, but because of his mercy. He washed away our sins, giving us a new birth and new life through the Holy Spirit.

TITUS 3:5 NLT

[God will] forever wipe the slate clean of their sins. Once sins are taken care of for good, there's no longer any need to offer sacrifices for them.

HEBREWS 10:17–18 MSG

You, Lord, are forgiving and good, abounding in love to all who call to you.

PSALM 86:5 NIV

And forgive us our sins; for we also forgive every one that is indebted to us. And lead us not into temptation; but deliver us from evil.

LUKE 11:4 KJV

"He himself bore our sins" in his body on the cross, so that we might die to sins and live for righteousness; "by his wounds you have been healed."

1 PETER 2:24 NIV

Christ had no sin, but God made him become sin so that in Christ we could become right with God.

2 CORINTHIANS 5:21 NCV

Then he turned toward the woman and said to Simon, "Do you see this woman? I came into your house. You did not give me any water for my feet, but she wet my feet with her tears and wiped them with her hair. You did not give me a kiss, but this woman, from the time I entered, has not stopped kissing my feet. You did not put oil on my head, but she has poured perfume on my feet. Therefore, I tell you, her many sins have been forgiven—as her great love has shown. But whoever has been forgiven little loves little." Then Jesus said to her, "Your sins are forgiven."

LUKE 7: 44–48 NIV

Don't repay evil for evil. Don't retaliate with insults when people insult you. Instead, pay them back with a blessing. That is what God has called you to do, and he will bless you for it.

1 PETER 3:9 NLT

I have hidden your word in my heart that I might not sin against you.

PSALM 119:11 NIV

"The LORD, the LORD, the compassionate and gracious God, slow to anger, abounding in love and faithfulness, maintaining love to thousands, and forgiving wickedness, rebellion and sin."

EXODUS 34:6–7 NIV

You are kind, God! Please have pity on me. You are always merciful! Please wipe away my sins. Wash me clean from all of my sin and guilt. I know about my sins, and I cannot forget my terrible guilt. You are really the one I have sinned against; I have disobeyed you and have done wrong. So it is right and fair for you to correct and punish me.

PSALM 51:1–4 CEV

The LORD is near to those who have a broken heart, and saves such as have a contrite spirit.

PSALM 34:18 NKJV

In him we have redemption through his blood, the forgiveness of sins, in accordance with the riches of God's grace that he lavished on us. With all wisdom and understanding.

EPHESIANS 1:7–8 NIV

Sin will not be your master, because you are not under law but under God's grace.

ROMANS 6:14 NCV

You hear our prayers. All people will come to you. Our guilt overwhelms us, but you forgive our sins. Happy are the people you choose and invite to stay in your court.

PSALM 65:2–4 NCV

All of us have sinned and fallen short of God's glory. But God treats us much better than we deserve, and because of Christ Jesus, he freely accepts us and sets us free from our sins.

ROMANS 3:23–24 CEV

"If they obey and serve him, they will spend the rest of their days in prosperity and their years in contentment."

JOB 36:11 NIV

God Gives
Me Courage

Dear Lord, give me the courage to boldly face my problems and to proudly share my faith. Help me to have absolute confidence in You alone—not in myself or in others. You created the entire world and everything in it, and that should be enough to give me the hope I need and the confidence to face anything. Thank You for Your goodness and the assurance You give me. Amen.

Wait on the LORD: be of good courage, and he shall strengthen thine heart: wait, I say, on the LORD.

PSALM 27:14 KJV

God did not give us a spirit that makes us afraid but a spirit of power and love and self-control.

2 TIMOTHY 1:7 NCV

Above all else, you must live in a way that brings honor to the good news about Christ. Then, whether I visit you or not, I will hear that all of you think alike. I will know that you are working together and that you are struggling side by side to get others to believe the good news. Be brave when you face your enemies. Your courage will show them that they are going to be destroyed, and it will show you that you will be saved.

PHILIPPIANS 1:27–28 CEV

And now, dear children, remain in fellowship with Christ so that when he returns, you will be full of courage and not shrink back from him in shame.

1 JOHN 2:28 NLT

Wait for the LORD's help. Be strong and brave, and wait for the LORD's help.

PSALM 27:14 NCV

When I asked for your help, you answered my prayer and gave me courage.

PSALM 138:3 CEV

So we say with confidence, "The Lord is my helper; I will not be afraid. What can mere mortals do to me?"

HEBREWS 13:6 NIV

In whom we have boldness and access with confidence by the faith of him.

EPHESIANS 3:12 KJV

"Be strong. Take courage. Don't be intimidated. Don't give them a second thought because GOD, your God, is striding ahead of you. He's right there with you. He won't let you down; he won't leave you."

DEUTERONOMY 31:6 MSG

Be strong and take heart, all you who hope in the LORD.

PSALM 31:24 NIV

She was thinking to herself, "If I can just put a finger on his robe, I'll get well." Jesus turned—caught her at it. Then he reassured her: "Courage, daughter. You took a risk of faith, and now you're well." The woman was well from then on.

MATTHEW 9:21–22 MSG

I have told you these things, so that in Me you may have [perfect] peace and confidence. In the world you have tribulation and trials and distress and frustration; but be of good cheer [take courage; be confident, certain, undaunted]! For I have overcome the world. [I have deprived it of power to harm you and have conquered it for you.]

JOHN 16:33 AMP

Wicked people run away when no one chases them, but those who live right are as brave as lions.

PROVERBS 28:1 CEV

Energize the limp hands, strengthen the rubbery knees. Tell fearful souls, "Courage! Take heart! GOD is here, right here, on his way to put things right and redress all wrongs. He's on his way! He'll save you!"

ISAIAH 35:3 MSG

"Only in returning to me and resting in me will you be saved. In quietness and confidence is your strength."

ISAIAH 30:15 NLT

After this prayer, the meeting place shook, and they were all filled with the Holy Spirit. Then they preached the word of God with boldness.

ACTS 4:31 NLT

Don't be so naive and self-confident. You're not exempt. You could fall flat on your face as easily as anyone else. Forget about self-confidence; it's useless. Cultivate God-confidence.

1 CORINTHIANS 10:12 MSG

This is the confidence we have in approaching God: that if we ask anything according to his will, he hears us.

1 JOHN 5:14 NIV

But Jesus immediately said to them: "Take courage! It is I. Don't be afraid."

MATTHEW 14:27 NIV

"But blessed are those who trust in the LORD and have made the LORD their hope and confidence."

JEREMIAH 17:7 NLT

And he did rescue us from mortal danger, and he will rescue us again. We have placed our confidence in him, and he will continue to rescue us.

2 CORINTHIANS 1:10 NLT

But you, LORD, are a shield around me, my glory, the One who lifts my head high.

PSALM 3:3 NIV

In his kindness God called you to share in his eternal glory by means of Christ Jesus. So after you have suffered a little while, he will restore, support, and strengthen you, and he will place you on a firm foundation.

1 PETER 5:10 NLT

"The LORD your God wins victory after victory and is always with you. He celebrates and sings because of you, and he will refresh your life with his love."

ZEPHANIAH 3:17 CEV

He has put his angels in charge of you to watch over you wherever you go. They will catch you in their hands so that you will not hit your foot on a rock.

PSALM 91:11–12 NCV

"So do not fear, for I am with you; do not be dismayed, for I am your God. I will strengthen you and help you; I will uphold you with my righteous right hand."

ISAIAH 41:10 NIV

Hezekiah rallied the people, saying, "Be strong! Take courage! Don't be intimidated by the king of Assyria and his troops—there are more on our side than on their side. He only has a bunch of mere men; we have our GOD to help us and fight for us!"

2 CHRONICLES 32:6–8 MSG

I've commanded you to be strong and brave. Don't ever be afraid or discouraged! I am the LORD your God, and I will be there to help you wherever you go.

JOSHUA 1:9 CEV

Be alert and on your guard; stand firm in your faith (your conviction respecting man's relationship to God and divine things, keeping the trust and holy fervor born of faith and a part of it). Act like men and be courageous; grow in strength!

1 CORINTHIANS 16:13 AMP

"Hear me, you who know what is right, you people who have taken my instruction to heart: Do not fear the reproach of mere mortals or be terrified by their insults."

ISAIAH 51:7 NIV

"Be brave and fight hard to protect our people and the towns of our LORD God. I pray he will do whatever pleases him."

1 CHRONICLES 19:13 CEV

I am the LORD, the one who encourages you. Why are you afraid of mere humans? They dry up and die like grass. I spread out the heavens and laid foundations for the earth. But you have forgotten me, your LORD and Creator. All day long you were afraid of those who were angry and hoped to abuse you. Where are they now? Everyone crying out in pain will be quickly set free; they will be rescued from the power of death and never go hungry. I will help them because I am your God, the LORD All-Powerful, who makes the ocean roar. I have told you what to say, and I will keep you safe in the palm of my hand. I spread out the heavens and laid foundations for the earth. Now I say, "Jerusalem, your people are mine."

ISAIAH 51:12–16 CEV

But Jesus looked at them and said, With men this is impossible, but all things are possible with God.

MATTHEW 19:26 AMP

It is better to trust and take refuge in the Lord than to put confidence in man. It is better to trust and take refuge in the Lord than to put confidence in princes.

PSALM 118:8–9 AMP

The LORD is good, a refuge in times of trouble. He cares for those who trust in him.

NAHUM 1:7 NIV

God has said this, and I have heard it over and over: God is strong.

PSALM 62:11 NCV

For the angel of the LORD is a guard; he surrounds and defends all who fear him. Taste and see that the LORD is good. Oh, the joys of those who take refuge in him!

PSALM 34:7–8 NLT

How great are His signs! And how mighty His wonders! His kingdom is an everlasting kingdom, and His dominion is from generation to generation.

DANIEL 4:3 AMP

Then Moses summoned Joshua and said to him in the presence of all Israel, "Be strong and courageous, for you must go with this people into the land that the LORD swore to their ancestors to give them, and you must divide it among them as their inheritance. The LORD himself goes before you and will be with you; he will never leave you nor forsake you. Do not be afraid; do not be discouraged."

DEUTERONOMY 31:7–8 NIV

GOD told me. . ."I'll tell you where to go and you'll go there. I'll tell you what to say and you'll say it. Don't be afraid of a soul. I'll be right there, looking after you."

JEREMIAH 1:8 MSG

"For you will be successful if you carefully obey the decrees and regulations that the LORD gave to Israel through Moses. Be strong and courageous; do not be afraid or lose heart!"

1 CHRONICLES 22:13 NLT

Is any thing too hard for the LORD?

GENESIS 18:14 KJV

" 'I will give peace to your country; you will lie down in peace, and no one will make you afraid. I will keep harmful animals out of your country, and armies will not pass through it.' "

LEVITICUS 26:6 NCV

God Gives Me Everything I Need

Dear God, You never stop providing for my needs and the desires of my heart. Sometimes I get so distracted by all of my wants that I forget to be thankful for the good things You have already given me—things like strength, comfort, peace, joy, hope, contentment, family, and friends. Please help me to grow a thankful heart and to always remember how generously You care for me. Amen.

The lions may grow weak and hungry, but those who seek the LORD lack no good thing.

PSALM 34:10 NIV

And my God shall supply all your need according to His riches in glory by Christ Jesus.

PHILIPPIANS 4:19 NKJV

He gives food to those who fear him; he always remembers his covenant.

PSALM 111:5 NLT

As for the rich in this world, charge them not to be proud and arrogant and contemptuous of others, nor to set their hopes on uncertain riches, but on God, Who richly and ceaselessly provides us with everything for [our] enjoyment.

1 TIMOTHY 6:17 AMP

Once I was young, and now I am old. Yet I have never seen the godly abandoned or their children begging for bread.

PSALM 37:25 NLT

May he give you what you want and make all your plans succeed.

PSALM 20:4 NCV

Do what the LORD wants, and he will give you your heart's desire.

PSALM 37:4 CEV

"For Jesus is the one referred to in the Scriptures, where it says, 'The stone that you builders rejected has now become the cornerstone.' There is salvation in no one else! God has given no other name under heaven by which we must be saved."

ACTS 4:11–12 NLT

Look closely at the sky! Stare at the earth. The sky will vanish like smoke; the earth will wear out like clothes. Everyone on this earth will die like flies. But my victory will last; my saving power never ends.

ISAIAH 51:6 CEV

He redeemed us in order that the blessing given to Abraham might come to the Gentiles through Christ Jesus, so that by faith we might receive the promise of the Spirit.

GALATIANS 3:14 NIV

"May the LORD bless you and keep you. May the LORD show you his kindness and have mercy on you. May the LORD watch over you and give you peace."

NUMBERS 6:24–26 NCV

"The LORD is my strength and my defense; he has become my salvation. He is my God, and I will praise him, my father's God, and I will exalt him."

EXODUS 15:2 NIV

"Therefore I tell you, do not worry about your life, what you will eat or drink; or about your body, what you will wear. Is not life more than food, and the body more than clothes? Look at the birds of the air; they do not sow or reap or store away in barns, and yet your heavenly Father feeds them. Are you not much more valuable than they? Can any one of you by worrying add a single hour to your life? And why do you worry about clothes? See how the flowers of the field grow. They do not labor or spin. Yet I tell you that not even Solomon in all his splendor was dressed like one of these. If that is how God clothes the grass of the field, which is here today and tomorrow is thrown into the fire, will he not much more clothe you—you of little faith? So do not worry, saying, 'What shall we eat?' or 'What shall we drink?' or 'What shall we wear?' For the pagans run after all these things, and your heavenly Father knows that you need them. But seek first his kingdom and his righteousness, and all these things will be given to you as well."

MATTHEW 6:25–33 NIV

People who are ruled by their desires think only of themselves. Everyone who is ruled by the Holy Spirit thinks about spiritual things.

ROMANS 8:5 CEV

And you also were included in Christ when you heard the message of truth, the gospel of your salvation. When you believed, you were marked in him with a seal, the promised Holy Spirit, who is a deposit guaranteeing our inheritance until the redemption of those who are God's possession—to the praise of his glory.

EPHESIANS 1:13–14 NIV

Trust in the LORD with all your heart, and lean not on your own understanding; in all your ways acknowledge Him, and He shall direct your paths. Do not be wise in your own eyes; fear the LORD and depart from evil. It will be health to your flesh, and strength to your bones.

PROVERBS 3:5–8 NKJV

God has done all this, so that we will look for him and reach out and find him. He isn't far from any of us, and he gives us the power to live, to move, and to be who we are. "We are his children," just as some of your poets have said.

ACTS 17:27–28 CEV

Give your burdens to the LORD, and he will take care of you. He will not permit the godly to slip and fall.

PSALM 55:22 NLT

"So do not fear, for I am with you; do not be dismayed, for I am your God. I will strengthen you and help you; I will uphold you with my righteous right hand."

ISAIAH 41:10 NIV

Fig trees may not grow figs, and there may be no grapes on the vines. There may be no olives growing and no food growing in the fields. There may be no sheep in the pens and no cattle in the barns. But I will still be glad in the LORD; I will rejoice in God my Savior. The Lord GOD is my strength. He makes me like a deer that does not stumble so I can walk on the steep mountains.

HABAKKUK 3:17–19 NCV

The LORD is my strength and shield. I trust him with all my heart. He helps me, and my heart is filled with joy. I burst out in songs of thanksgiving.

PSALM 28:7 NLT

The instructions of the LORD are perfect, reviving the soul. The decrees of the LORD are trustworthy, making wise the simple.

PSALM 19:7 NLT

Then Jesus turned to his disciples and said, "God blesses you who are poor, for the Kingdom of God is yours. God blesses you who are hungry now, for you will be satisfied. God blesses you who weep now, for in due time you will laugh. What blessings await you when people hate you and exclude you and mock you and curse you as evil because you follow the Son of Man. When that happens, be happy! Yes, leap for joy! For a great reward awaits you in heaven. And remember, their ancestors treated the ancient prophets that same way."

LUKE 6:20–23 NLT

If they plant to satisfy their sinful selves, their sinful selves will bring them ruin. But if they plant to please the Spirit, they will receive eternal life from the Spirit. We must not become tired of doing good. We will receive our harvest of eternal life at the right time if we do not give up. When we have the opportunity to help anyone, we should do it. But we should give special attention to those who are in the family of believers.

GALATIANS 6:8–10 NCV

God Gives
Me Hope

Heavenly Father, I put my hope and trust in You because I know that You will never fail me. I only need to look at Your Word to know that You keep Your promises to those who love You and seek Your will. You will never disappoint or let me down.
I can place all of my expectations and dreams in Your care, knowing that You have my best interests at heart. Thank You for giving me hope. Amen.

For I know the thoughts that I think toward you, says the LORD, thoughts of peace and not of evil, to give you a future and a hope.

JEREMIAH 29:11 NKJV

Since we have such [glorious] hope (such joyful and confident expectation), we speak very freely and openly and fearlessly.

2 CORINTHIANS 3:12 AMP

You are my refuge and my shield; your word is my source of hope.

PSALM 119:114 NLT

But the LORD looks after those who fear him, those who put their hope in his love.

PSALM 33:18 NCV

Moreover [let us also be full of joy now!] let us exult and triumph in our troubles and rejoice in our sufferings, knowing that pressure and affliction and hardship produce patient and unswerving endurance. And endurance (fortitude) develops maturity of character (approved faith and tried integrity). And character [of this sort] produces [the habit of] joyful and confident hope of eternal salvation. Such hope never disappoints or deludes or shames us, for God's love has been poured out in our hearts through the Holy Spirit Who has been given to us.

ROMANS 5:3–5 AMP

But since we belong to the day, let us be sober, putting on faith and love as a breastplate, and the hope of salvation as a helmet.

1 THESSALONIANS 5:8 NIV

Instead, you must worship Christ as Lord of your life. And if someone asks about your Christian hope, always be ready to explain it.

1 PETER 3:15 NLT

Then they will have the hope of eternal life that God promised long ago. And God never tells a lie!

TITUS 1:2 CEV

But we have the true hope that comes from being made right with God, and by the Spirit we wait eagerly for this hope.

GALATIANS 5:5 NCV

But Christ is faithful as the Son over God's house. And we are his house, if indeed we hold firmly to our confidence and the hope in which we glory.

HEBREWS 3:6 NIV

I pray that God, the source of hope, will fill you completely with joy and peace because you trust in him. Then you will overflow with confident hope through the power of the Holy Spirit.

ROMANS 15:13 NLT

These two things cannot change: God cannot lie when he makes a promise, and he cannot lie when he makes an oath. These things encourage us who came to God for safety. They give us strength to hold on to the hope we have been given. We have this hope as an anchor for the soul, sure and strong. It enters behind the curtain in the Most Holy Place in heaven.

HEBREWS 6:18–19 NCV

Through Christ you have come to trust in God. And you have placed your faith and hope in God because he raised Christ from the dead and gave him great glory.

1 PETER 1:21 NLT

"And I have the same hope in God as these men themselves have, that there will be a resurrection of both the righteous and the wicked."

ACTS 24:15 NIV

And we desire that each one of you show the same diligence to the full assurance of hope until the end.

HEBREWS 6:11 NKJV

For in this hope we were saved. But hope that is seen is no hope at all. Who hopes for what they already have? But if we hope for what we do not yet have, we wait for it patiently.

ROMANS 8:24–25 NIV

LORD, I hope for Your salvation, and I do Your
commandments.

PSALM 119:166 NKJV

I pray also that you will have greater understanding in
your heart so you will know the hope to which he has
called us and that you will know how rich and glorious
are the blessings God has promised his holy people.

EPHESIANS 1:18 NCV

I honestly expect and hope that I will never do
anything to be ashamed of. Whether I live or die, I
always want to be as brave as I am now and bring
honor to Christ.

PHILIPPIANS 1:20 CEV

Remember your word to your servant, for you have
given me hope.

PSALM 119:49 NIV

Why are you cast down, O my soul? And why are you
disquieted within me? Hope in God; for I shall yet
praise Him, the help of my countenance and my God.

PSALM 42:11 NKJV

Which come from your confident hope of what God
has reserved for you in heaven. You have had this
expectation ever since you first heard the truth of
the Good News.

COLOSSIANS 1:5 NLT

But God will never forget the needy; the hope of the afflicted will never perish.

PSALM 9:18 NIV

My dear friends, we are already God's children, though what we will be hasn't yet been seen. But we do know that when Christ returns, we will be like him, because we will see him as he truly is. This hope makes us keep ourselves holy, just as Christ is holy.

1 JOHN 3:2–3 CEV

We call Abraham "father" not because he got God's attention by living like a saint, but because God made something out of Abraham when he was a nobody. Isn't that what we've always read in Scripture, God saying to Abraham, "I set you up as father of many peoples"? Abraham was first named "father" and then became a father because he dared to trust God to do what only God could do: raise the dead to life, with a word make something out of nothing. When everything was hopeless, Abraham believed anyway, deciding to live not on the basis of what he saw he couldn't do but on what God said he would do. And so he was made father of a multitude of peoples. God himself said to him, "You're going to have a big family, Abraham!"

ROMANS 4:17–18 MSG

Praise be to the God and Father of our Lord Jesus Christ! In his great mercy he has given us new birth into a living hope through the resurrection of Jesus Christ from the dead.

1 PETER 1:3 NIV

"Blessed is the man who trusts in the LORD, and whose hope is the LORD."

JEREMIAH 17:7 NKJV

All of you are part of the same body. There is only one Spirit of God, just as you were given one hope when you were chosen to be God's people.

EPHESIANS 4:4 CEV

The Lord is my portion or share, says my living being (my inner self); therefore will I hope in Him and wait expectantly for Him. The Lord is good to those who wait hopefully and expectantly for Him, to those who seek Him [inquire of and for Him and require Him by right of necessity and on the authority of God's word]. It is good that one should hope in and wait quietly for the salvation (the safety and ease) of the Lord.

LAMENTATIONS 3:24–26 AMP

"I have the same hope in God that they have—the hope that all people, good and bad, will surely be raised from the dead."

ACTS 24:15 NCV

Or does He speak certainly and entirely for our sakes? [Assuredly] it is written for our sakes, because the plowman ought to plow in hope, and the thresher ought to thresh in expectation of partaking of the harvest.

1 CORINTHIANS 9:10 AMP

Happy are those who are helped by the God of Jacob. Their hope is in the LORD their God.

PSALM 146:5 NCV

Because of our faith, Christ has brought us into this place of undeserved privilege where we now stand, and we confidently and joyfully look forward to sharing God's glory.

ROMANS 5:2 NLT

You will be secure, because there is hope; you will look about you and take your rest in safety. You will lie down, with no one to make you afraid, and many will court your favor.

JOB 11:18–19 NIV

Show me your ways, LORD, teach me your paths. Guide me in your truth and teach me, for you are God my Savior, and my hope is in you all day long. Remember, LORD, your great mercy and love, for they are from of old.

PSALM 25:4–6 NIV

And the Scriptures were written to teach and encourage us by giving us hope.

ROMANS 15:4 CEV

And so faith, hope, love abide [faith—conviction and belief respecting man's relation to God and divine things; hope—joyful and confident expectation of eternal salvation; love—true affection for God and man, growing out of God's love for and in us], these three; but the greatest of these is love.

1 CORINTHIANS 13:13 AMP

Remember that in the past you were without Christ. You were not citizens of Israel, and you had no part in the agreements with the promise that God made to his people. You had no hope, and you did not know God. But now in Christ Jesus, you who were far away from God are brought near through the blood of Christ's death. Christ himself is our peace. He made both Jewish people and those who are not Jews one people. They were separated as if there were a wall between them, but Christ broke down that wall of hate by giving his own body.

EPHESIANS 2:12–14 NCV

God Gives
Me Joy

Dear Lord, I find myself seeking happiness most of the time, but I know that joy should be my goal. Happiness quickly comes and goes, depending on temporary situations, but joy is dependent on the state of my heart. Let my heart be filled with the joy that comes from You, my heavenly Father, and help me to share that joy with everyone I meet. No matter what happens in my life, I want to praise You with my thoughts, my actions, and my words. Amen.

Shout to the LORD, all the earth. Serve the LORD with joy; come before him with singing.

PSALM 100:1–2 NCV

"I am coming to you now, but I say these things while I am still in the world, so that they may have the full measure of my joy within them."

JOHN 17:13 NIV

Not that we have dominion [over you] and lord it over your faith, but [rather that we work with you as] fellow laborers [to promote] your joy, for in [your] faith (in your strong and welcome conviction or belief that Jesus is the Messiah, through Whom we obtain eternal salvation in the kingdom of God) you stand firm.

2 CORINTHIANS 1:24 AMP

Is anyone among you in trouble? Let them pray. Is anyone happy? Let them sing songs of praise.

JAMES 5:13 NIV

For our heart shall rejoice in Him, because we have trusted in His holy name.

PSALM 33:21 NKJV

Singing psalms and hymns and spiritual songs among yourselves, and making music to the Lord in your hearts.

EPHESIANS 5:19 NLT

The LORD is my strength and my shield; my heart trusted in Him, and I am helped; therefore my heart greatly rejoices, and with my song I will praise Him.

PSALM 28:7 NKJV

Always be full of joy in the Lord. I say it again—rejoice!

PHILIPPIANS 4:4 NLT

Until now you have not asked for anything in my name. Ask and you will receive, and your joy will be complete.

JOHN 16:24 NIV

Be glad in the LORD and rejoice, you righteous; and shout for joy, all you upright in heart!

PSALM 32:11 NKJV

As sorrowful, yet always rejoicing; as poor, yet making many rich; as having nothing, and yet possessing all things.

2 CORINTHIANS 6:10 KJV

So the ransomed of the LORD shall return, and come to Zion with singing, with everlasting joy on their heads. They shall obtain joy and gladness; sorrow and sighing shall flee away.

ISAIAH 51:11 NKJV

I will sing for joy in GOD, explode in praise from deep in my soul! He dressed me up in a suit of salvation, he outfitted me in a robe of righteousness, as a bridegroom who puts on a tuxedo and a bride a jeweled tiara. For as the earth bursts with spring wildflowers, and as a garden cascades with blossoms, so the Master, GOD, brings righteousness into full bloom and puts praise on display before the nations.

ISAIAH 61:10 MSG

"The master answered, 'You did well. You are a good and loyal servant. Because you were loyal with small things, I will let you care for much greater things. Come and share my joy with me.' "

MATTHEW 25:21 NCV

If you are cheerful, you feel good; if you are sad, you hurt all over.

PROVERBS 17:22 CEV

All the days of the desponding and afflicted are made evil [by anxious thoughts and forebodings], but he who has a glad heart has a continual feast [regardless of circumstances].

PROVERBS 15:15 AMP

Our LORD, let your worshipers rejoice and be glad. They love you for saving them, so let them always say, "The LORD is wonderful!"

PSALM 40:16 CEV

I will shout for joy when I sing praises to you. You have saved me.

PSALM 71:23 NCV

All the days of the afflicted are evil, but he who is of a merry heart has a continual feast.

PROVERBS 15:15 NKJV

"This is what I want you to do: Ask the Father for whatever is in keeping with the things I've revealed to you. Ask in my name, according to my will, and he'll most certainly give it to you. Your joy will be a river overflowing its banks!"

JOHN 16:24 MSG

You will show me the way of life, granting me the joy of your presence and the pleasures of living with you forever.

PSALM 16:11 NLT

Give thanks to the LORD, for he is good! His faithful love endures forever. Cry out, "Save us, O God of our salvation! Gather and rescue us from among the nations, so we can thank your holy name and rejoice and praise you." Praise the LORD, the God of Israel, who lives from everlasting to everlasting! And all the people shouted "Amen!" and praised the LORD.

1 CHRONICLES 16:34–36 NLT

Honor and majesty are [found] in His presence;
strength and joy are [found] in His sanctuary.

1 CHRONICLES 16:27 AMP

But the fruit of the Spirit is love, joy, peace,
longsuffering, kindness, goodness, faithfulness,
gentleness, self-control. Against such there is no law.

GALATIANS 5:22–23 NKJV

Oh! Teach us to live well! Teach us to live wisely and
well! Come back, GOD—how long do we have to
wait?—and treat your servants with kindness for a
change. Surprise us with love at daybreak; then we'll
skip and dance all the day long. Make up for the bad
times with some good times; we've seen enough evil
to last a lifetime. Let your servants see what you're
best at—the ways you rule and bless your children.
And let the loveliness of our Lord, our God, rest on
us, confirming the work that we do. Oh, yes. Affirm
the work that we do!

PSALM 90:12–17 MSG

If you obey me, I will keep loving you, just as my
Father keeps loving me, because I have obeyed
him. I have told you this to make you as completely
happy as I am.

JOHN 15:10–11 CEV

"And my spirit rejoices in God my Savior."

LUKE 1:47 NIV

You have turned my sorrow into joyful dancing. No
longer am I sad and wearing sackcloth.

PSALM 30:11 CEV

I will celebrate and be joyful because you, LORD,
have saved me. Every bone in my body will shout:
"No one is like the LORD!" You protect the helpless
from those in power; you save the poor and needy
from those who hurt them.

PSALM 35:9–10 CEV

I will praise you as long as I live. I will lift up my
hands in prayer to your name. I will be content as
if I had eaten the best foods. My lips will sing, and
my mouth will praise you. I remember you while I'm
lying in bed; I think about you through the night.

PSALM 63:4–6 NCV

Let the heavens rejoice, and let the earth be glad;
let the sea roar, and all its fullness; let the field
be joyful, and all that is in it. Then all the trees of
the woods will rejoice before the LORD. For He is
coming, for He is coming to judge the earth. He shall
judge the world with righteousness, and the peoples
with His truth.

PSALM 96:11–13 NKJV

God Gives
Me Strength

Heavenly Father, I don't think that I always understand just how mighty You really are. Sometimes I feel too weak, too young, or too overwhelmed to deal with hard situations.

When I'm going through difficult times, please remind me of Your willingness and ability to give me the strength that I need to face anything and overcome whatever is troubling me. I only need to call out and You are there, supporting me and providing all the strength that I need. Amen.

I know how to live when I am poor, and I know how to live when I have plenty. I have learned the secret of being happy at any time in everything that happens, when I have enough to eat and when I go hungry, when I have more than I need and when I do not have enough. I can do all things through Christ, because he gives me strength.

PHILIPPIANS 4:12–13 NCV

My body and mind may fail, but you are my strength and my choice forever.

PSALM 73:26 CEV

"The righteous keep moving forward, and those with clean hands become stronger and stronger."

JOB 17:9 NLT

That you may walk worthy of the Lord, fully pleasing Him, being fruitful in every good work and increasing in the knowledge of God; strengthened with all might, according to His glorious power, for all patience and longsuffering with joy.

COLOSSIANS 1:10–11 NKJV

God is awesome in his sanctuary. The God of Israel gives power and strength to his people. Praise be to God!

PSALM 68:35 NLT

In conclusion, be strong in the Lord [be empowered through your union with Him]; draw your strength from Him [that strength which His boundless might provides]. Put on God's whole armor [the armor of a heavy-armed soldier which God supplies], that you may be able successfully to stand up against [all] the strategies and the deceits of the devil.

EPHESIANS 6:10–11 AMP

"Wealth and honor come from you; you are the ruler of all things. In your hands are strength and power to exalt and give strength to all."

1 CHRONICLES 29:12 NIV

He gives strength to the weary and increases the power of the weak.

ISAIAH 40:29 NIV

Each time he said, "My grace is all you need. My power works best in weakness." So now I am glad to boast about my weaknesses, so that the power of Christ can work through me.

2 CORINTHIANS 12:9 NLT

The LORD is my rock, my protection, my Savior. My God is my rock. I can run to him for safety. He is my shield and my saving strength, my defender.

PSALM 18:2 NCV

He was amazed to see that no one intervened to help the oppressed. So he himself stepped in to save them with his strong arm, and his justice sustained him. He put on righteousness as his body armor and placed the helmet of salvation on his head. He clothed himself with a robe of vengeance and wrapped himself in a cloak of divine passion.

ISAIAH 59:16–17 NLT

The word of the LORD came to Abram in a vision, saying, "Do not be afraid, Abram. I am your shield, your exceedingly great reward."

GENESIS 15:1–2 NKJV

But You, O Lord, are a shield for me, my glory, and the lifter of my head.

PSALM 3:3 AMP

He will cover you with his feathers, and under his wings you can hide. His truth will be your shield and protection.

PSALM 91:4 NCV

The name of the LORD is a strong fortress; the godly run to him and are safe.

PROVERBS 18:10 NLT

For the Kingdom of God is not just a lot of talk; it is living by God's power.

1 CORINTHIANS 4:20 NLT

If this is so, then the Lord knows how to rescue the godly from trials and to hold the unrighteous for punishment on the day of judgment.

2 PETER 2:9 NIV

"Watch and pray, lest you enter into temptation. The spirit indeed is willing, but the flesh is weak."

MATTHEW 26:41 NKJV

The only temptation that has come to you is that which everyone has. But you can trust God, who will not permit you to be tempted more than you can stand. But when you are tempted, he will also give you a way to escape so that you will be able to stand it.

1 CORINTHIANS 10:13 NCV

The night is nearly over; the day is almost here. So let us put aside the deeds of darkness and put on the armor of light.

ROMANS 13:12 NIV

We live in this world, but we don't act like its people or fight our battles with the weapons of this world. Instead, we use God's power that can destroy fortresses. We destroy arguments and every bit of pride that keeps anyone from knowing God. We capture people's thoughts and make them obey Christ.

2 CORINTHIANS 10:3–5 CEV

For since the creation of the world His invisible attributes are clearly seen, being understood by the things that are made, even His eternal power and Godhead, so that they are without excuse.

ROMANS 1:20 NKJV

"But you will receive power when the Holy Spirit comes upon you. And you will be my witnesses, telling people about me everywhere—in Jerusalem, throughout Judea, in Samaria, and to the ends of the earth."

ACTS 1:8 NLT

That's why I am suffering now. But I am not ashamed! I know the one I have faith in, and I am sure that he can guard until the last day what he has trusted me with. Now follow the example of the correct teaching I gave you, and let the faith and love of Christ Jesus be your model.

2 TIMOTHY 1:12–13 CEV

These trials will show that your faith is genuine. It is being tested as fire tests and purifies gold—though your faith is far more precious than mere gold. So when your faith remains strong through many trials, it will bring you much praise and glory and honor on the day when Jesus Christ is revealed to the whole world.

1 PETER 1:7 NLT

And lead (bring) us not into temptation, but deliver us from the evil one. For Yours is the kingdom and the power and the glory forever. Amen.

MATTHEW 6:13 AMP

Then Jesus spoke to them again, saying, "I am the light of the world. He who follows Me shall not walk in darkness, but have the light of life."

JOHN 8:12 NKJV

We have come to share in Christ, if indeed we hold our original conviction firmly to the very end.

HEBREWS 3:14 NIV

Yes, though I walk through the [deep, sunless] valley of the shadow of death, I will fear or dread no evil, for You are with me; Your rod [to protect] and Your staff [to guide], they comfort me.

PSALM 23:4 AMP

I sought the LORD, and He heard me, and delivered me from all my fears.

PSALM 34:4 NKJV

My dear friends, you always obeyed when I was with you. Now that I am away, you should obey even more. So work with fear and trembling to discover what it really means to be saved. God is working in you to make you willing and able to obey him.

PHILIPPIANS 2:12–13 CEV

"The LORD your God is with you, the Mighty Warrior who saves. He will take great delight in you; in his love he will no longer rebuke you, but will rejoice over you with singing."

ZEPHANIAH 3:17 NIV

Now to Him who is able to do exceedingly abundantly above all that we ask or think, according to the power that works in us, to Him be glory in the church by Christ Jesus to all generations, forever and ever. Amen.

EPHESIANS 3:20–21 NKJV

The holy LORD God of Israel had told all of you, "I will keep you safe if you turn back to me and calm down. I will make you strong if you quietly trust me."

ISAIAH 30:15 CEV

[For it is He] Who rescued and saved us from such a perilous death, and He will still rescue and save us; in and on Him we have set our hope (our joyful and confident expectation) that He will again deliver us [from danger and destruction and draw us to Himself].

2 CORINTHIANS 1:10 AMP

This is the confidence we have in approaching God: that if we ask anything according to his will, he hears us.

1 JOHN 5:14 NIV

By innocence and purity, knowledge and spiritual insight, longsuffering and patience, kindness, in the Holy Spirit, in unfeigned love; by [speaking] the word of truth, in the power of God, with the weapons of righteousness for the right hand [to attack] and for the left hand [to defend].

2 CORINTHIANS 6:6–7 AMP

But those who hope in the LORD will renew their strength. They will soar on wings like eagles; they will run and not grow weary, they will walk and not be faint.

ISAIAH 40:31 NIV

Though he fall, he shall not be utterly cast down; for the LORD upholds him with His hand.

PSALM 37:24 NKJV

Therefore, since we are surrounded by such a huge crowd of witnesses to the life of faith, let us strip off every weight that slows us down, especially the sin that so easily trips us up. And let us run with endurance the race God has set before us. We do this by keeping our eyes on Jesus, the champion who initiates and perfects our faith. Because of the joy awaiting him, he endured the cross, disregarding its shame. Now he is seated in the place of honor beside God's throne.

HEBREWS 12:1–2 NLT

God Has a Plan for Me

Dear Lord, sometimes I forget
that my life is not my own.
You have a plan for me—a special
plan for my life that was in place
even before I was born.
Although I may not know what
that plan is right now, I trust that You
have my best interests at heart. Lord,
take my will and my plans and make
them Yours. I want my life to glorify
You in everything. Amen.

"For I know the plans I have for you," declares the LORD, "plans to prosper you and not to harm you, plans to give you hope and a future."

JEREMIAH 29:11 NIV

Lean on, trust in, and be confident in the Lord with all your heart and mind and do not rely on your own insight or understanding. In all your ways know, recognize, and acknowledge Him, and He will direct and make straight and plain your paths.

PROVERBS 3:5–6 AMP

"If this is true, let me know what your plans are, then I can obey and continue to please you. And don't forget that you have chosen this nation to be your own." The LORD said, "I will go with you and give you peace."

EXODUS 33:13–14 CEV

But God led his people out like sheep and he guided them like a flock through the desert. He led them to safety so they had nothing to fear.

PSALM 78:52–53 NCV

The LORD is my shepherd, I lack nothing. He makes me lie down in green pastures, he leads me beside quiet waters, he refreshes my soul. He guides me along the right paths for his name's sake.

PSALM 23:1–3 NIV

You said to me, "I will point out the road that you should follow. I will be your teacher and watch over you."

PSALM 32:8 CEV

For that is what God is like. He is our God forever and ever, and he will guide us until we die.

PSALM 48:14 NLT

Your kingdom is an everlasting kingdom, and Your dominion endures throughout all generations. The LORD upholds all who fall, and raises up all who are bowed down.

PSALM 145:13–14 NKJV

Commit to the LORD whatever you do, and he will establish your plans.

PROVERBS 16:3 NIV

Do not fret or have any anxiety about anything, but in every circumstance and in everything, by prayer and petition (definite requests), with thanksgiving, continue to make your wants known to God. And God's peace [shall be yours, that tranquil state of a soul assured of its salvation through Christ, and so fearing nothing from God and being content with its earthly lot of whatever sort that is, that peace] which transcends all understanding shall garrison and mount guard over your hearts and minds in Christ Jesus.

PHILIPPIANS 4:6–7 AMP

I tell you not to worry about your life. Don't worry about having something to eat, drink, or wear. Isn't life more than food or clothing? Look at the birds in the sky! They don't plant or harvest. They don't even store grain in barns. Yet your Father in heaven takes care of them. Aren't you worth more than birds?

MATTHEW 6:25–26 CEV

Jesus has the power of God, by which he has given us everything we need to live and to serve God. We have these things because we know him. Jesus called us by his glory and goodness.

2 PETER 1:3 NCV

Rather, you must grow in the grace and knowledge of our Lord and Savior Jesus Christ. All glory to him, both now and forever! Amen.

2 PETER 3:18 NLT

All you who fear GOD, how blessed you are! How happily you walk on his smooth straight road! You worked hard and deserve all you've got coming. Enjoy the blessing! Revel in the goodness!

PSALM 128:2 MSG

Moreover, when God gives someone wealth and possessions, and the ability to enjoy them, to accept their lot and be happy in their toil—this is a gift of God.

ECCLESIASTES 5:19 NIV

Humility is the fear of the LORD; its wages are riches and honor and life.

PROVERBS 22:4 NIV

And the Lord your God will make you abundantly prosperous in every work of your hand, in the fruit of your body, of your cattle, of your land, for good; for the Lord will again delight in prospering you, as He took delight in your fathers.

DEUTERONOMY 30:9 AMP

And also that every man should eat and drink and enjoy the good of all his labor—it is the gift of God.

ECCLESIASTES 3:13 AMP

In their hearts humans plan their course, but the LORD establishes their steps.

PROVERBS 16:9 NIV

Hear counsel, receive instruction, and accept correction, that you may be wise in the time to come. Many plans are in a man's mind, but it is the Lord's purpose for him that will stand.

PROVERBS 19:20–21 AMP

Fools think they know what is best, but a sensible person listens to advice.

PROVERBS 12:15 CEV

"Abide in Me, and I in you. As the branch cannot bear fruit of itself, unless it abides in the vine, neither can you, unless you abide in Me. I am the vine, you are the branches. He who abides in Me, and I in him, bears much fruit; for without Me you can do nothing."

JOHN 15:4–5 NKJV

You guide me with your advice, and later you will receive me in honor.

PSALM 73:24 NCV

Today I am giving you a choice. You can choose life and success or death and disaster. I am commanding you to be loyal to the LORD, to live the way he has told you, and to obey his laws and teachings.

DEUTERONOMY 30:15–16 CEV

In Him we have redemption through His blood, the forgiveness of sins, according to the riches of His grace which He made to abound toward us in all wisdom and prudence, having made known to us the mystery of His will, according to His good pleasure which He purposed in Himself, that in the dispensation of the fullness of the times He might gather together in one all things in Christ, both which are in heaven and which are on earth—in Him.

EPHESIANS 1:7–10 NKJV

The plan of the Holy One of Israel—let it approach, let it come into view, so we may know it.

ISAIAH 5:19 NIV

Don't copy the behavior and customs of this world, but let God transform you into a new person by changing the way you think. Then you will learn to know God's will for you, which is good and pleasing and perfect.

ROMANS 12:2 NLT

Be very careful, then, how you live—not as unwise but as wise, making the most of every opportunity, because the days are evil. Therefore do not be foolish, but understand what the Lord's will is. . . . Be filled with the Spirit.

EPHESIANS 5:15–18 NIV

Love from the center of who you are; don't fake it. Run for dear life from evil; hold on for dear life to good. Be good friends who love deeply; practice playing second fiddle. Don't burn out; keep yourselves fueled and aflame. Be alert servants of the Master, cheerfully expectant. Don't quit in hard times; pray all the harder. Help needy Christians; be inventive in hospitality.

ROMANS 12:9–13 MSG

If you need wisdom, ask our generous God, and he will give it to you. He will not rebuke you for asking.

JAMES 1:5 NLT

God
Hears Me

Dear God, thank You for always being there, for listening to me talk about the big and small things in my life. You are never too busy to listen to what I have to say, and nothing is too insignificant for You to care. Sometimes I forget that You are there, ready and waiting to hear from me—about my troubles or my joy over something wonderful. Remind me of Your enduring presence, Lord. Amen.

As bad as you are, you still know how to give good gifts to your children. But your heavenly Father is even more ready to give good things to people who ask.

MATTHEW 7:11 CEV

"In that day you will not ask me for anything. I tell you the truth, my Father will give you anything you ask for in my name. Until now you have not asked for anything in my name. Ask and you will receive, so that your joy will be the fullest possible joy."

JOHN 16:23–24 NCV

"Here's what I want you to do: Find a quiet, secluded place so you won't be tempted to role-play before God. Just be there as simply and honestly as you can manage. The focus will shift from you to God, and you will begin to sense his grace. The world is full of so-called prayer warriors who are prayer-ignorant. They're full of formulas and programs and advice, peddling techniques for getting what you want from God. Don't fall for that nonsense. This is your Father you are dealing with, and he knows better than you what you need. With a God like this loving you, you can pray very simply."

MATTHEW 6:6–11 MSG

Listen to my words, LORD, consider my lament. Hear my cry for help, my King and my God, for to you I pray. In the morning, LORD, you hear my voice; in the morning I lay my requests before you and wait expectantly.

PSALM 5:1–3 NIV

Morning, noon, and night I cry out in my distress, and the LORD hears my voice.

PSALM 55:17 NLT

The LORD will hear your crying, and he will comfort you. When he hears you, he will help you.

ISAIAH 30:19 NCV

Pray without ceasing.

1 THESSALONIANS 5:17 KJV

God will answer your prayers, and you will keep the promises you made to him.

JOB 22:27 CEV

And pray in the Spirit on all occasions with all kinds of prayers and requests. With this in mind, be alert and always keep on praying for all the Lord's people.

EPHESIANS 6:18 NIV

I waited patiently for the LORD. He turned to me and heard my cry.

PSALM 40:1 NCV

"Even he rendered a just decision in the end. So don't you think God will surely give justice to his chosen people who cry out to him day and night? Will he keep putting them off?"

LUKE 18:7 NLT

Rejoicing in hope, patient in tribulation, continuing steadfastly in prayer.

ROMANS 12:12 NKJV

"If you have faith when you pray, you will be given whatever you ask for."

MATTHEW 21:22 CEV

If My people, who are called by My name, shall humble themselves, pray, seek, crave, and require of necessity My face and turn from their wicked ways, then will I hear from heaven, forgive their sin, and heal their land.

2 CHRONICLES 7:14 AMP

"Then you will call my name. You will come to me and pray to me, and I will listen to you. You will search for me. And when you search for me with all your heart, you will find me!"

JEREMIAH 29:12–13 NCV

GOD's there, listening for all who pray, for all who pray and mean it.

PSALM 145:18 MSG

So let us come boldly to the throne of our gracious God. There we will receive his mercy, and we will find grace to help us when we need it most.

HEBREWS 4:16 NLT

The LORD detests the sacrifice of the wicked, but he delights in the prayers of the upright.

PROVERBS 15:8 NLT

I will provide for their needs before they ask, and I will help them while they are still asking for help.

ISAIAH 65:24 NCV

And this is the confidence (the assurance, the privilege of boldness) which we have in Him: [we are sure] that if we ask anything (make any request) according to His will (in agreement with His own plan), He listens to and hears us. And if (since) we [positively] know that He listens to us in whatever we ask, we also know [with settled and absolute knowledge] that we have [granted us as our present possessions] the requests made of Him.

1 JOHN 5:14–15 AMP

In certain ways we are weak, but the Spirit is here to help us. For example, when we don't know what to pray for, the Spirit prays for us in ways that cannot be put into words.

ROMANS 8:26 CEV

So, I want the men everywhere to pray, lifting up their hands in a holy manner, without anger and arguments.

1 TIMOTHY 2:8 NCV

Don't worry about anything, but pray about everything. With thankful hearts offer up your prayers and requests to God. Then, because you belong to Christ Jesus, God will bless you with peace that no one can completely understand. And this peace will control the way you think and feel.

PHILIPPIANS 4:6–7 CEV

Let them give thanks to the LORD for his love and
for the miracles he does for people.

PSALM 107:15 NCV

By day the LORD directs his love, at night his song is
with me—a prayer to the God of my life.

PSALM 42:8 NIV

Again I tell you, if two of you on earth agree
(harmonize together, make a symphony together)
about whatever [anything and everything] they may
ask, it will come to pass and be done for them by
My Father in heaven. For wherever two or three are
gathered (drawn together as My followers) in (into)
My name, there I AM in the midst of them.

MATTHEW 18:19–20 AMP

The persons they mistreated had prayed for help,
until God answered their prayers.

JOB 34:28 CEV

If you are having trouble, you should pray. And if
you are feeling good, you should sing praises. If you
are sick, ask the church leaders to come and pray for
you. Ask them to put olive oil on you in the name
of the Lord. If you have faith when you pray for sick
people, they will get well. The Lord will heal them,
and if they have sinned, he will forgive them.

JAMES 5:13–15 CEV

We worship you, Lord, and we should always pray whenever we find out that we have sinned. Then we won't be swept away by a raging flood.

PSALM 32:6 CEV

"You're familiar with the old written law, 'Love your friend,' and its unwritten companion, 'Hate your enemy.' I'm challenging that. I'm telling you to love your enemies. Let them bring out the best in you, not the worst. When someone gives you a hard time, respond with the energies of prayer, for then you are working out of your true selves, your God-created selves."

MATTHEW 5:43–44 MSG

For this reason I am telling you, whatever you ask for in prayer, believe (trust and be confident) that it is granted to you, and you will [get it].

MARK 11:24 AMP

You, LORD, heard my crying, and those hateful people had better leave me alone. You have answered my prayer and my plea for mercy.

PSALM 6:8–9 CEV

But certainly God has heard me; He has given heed to the voice of my prayer. Blessed be God, Who has not rejected my prayer nor removed His mercy and loving-kindness from being [as it always is] with me.

PSALM 66:19–20 AMP

"When you call on me, when you come and pray to me, I'll listen."

JEREMIAH 29:12 MSG

But we will give ourselves continually to prayer, and to the ministry of the word.

ACTS 6:4 KJV

Rejoicing in hope, patient in tribulation, continuing steadfastly in prayer.

ROMANS 12:12 NKJV

And pray in the Spirit on all occasions with all kinds of prayers and requests. With this in mind, be alert and always keep on praying for all the Lord's people.

EPHESIANS 6:18 NIV

Ask, and you will receive. Search, and you will find. Knock, and the door will be opened for you. Everyone who asks will receive. Everyone who searches will find. And the door will be opened for everyone who knocks.

MATTHEW 7:7–8 CEV

Well then, what shall I do? I will pray in the spirit, and I will also pray in words I understand. I will sing in the spirit, and I will also sing in words I understand.

1 CORINTHIANS 14:15 NLT

God Is Always with Me

Heavenly Father, in the Bible it says that You will never leave me or forsake me. Please remind me of Your Word when I am feeling lonely or when it seems like no one cares about me. And when I feel like You are far away, remind me that it's not because You have left me but because I am not reaching out to find You. Thank You for Your security, Lord. It's comforting to know that nothing can separate me from Your presence or Your love. Amen.

Is there anyplace I can go to avoid your Spirit? to be out of your sight? If I climb to the sky, you're there! If I go underground, you're there! If I flew on morning's wings to the far western horizon, you'd find me in a minute—you're already there waiting! Then I said to myself, "Oh, he even sees me in the dark! At night I'm immersed in the light!" It's a fact: darkness isn't dark to you; night and day, darkness and light, they're all the same to you.

PSALM 139:7–10 MSG

My old self has been crucified with Christ. It is no longer I who live, but Christ lives in me. So I live in this earthly body by trusting in the Son of God, who loved me and gave himself for me.

GALATIANS 2:20 NLT

Know, recognize, and understand therefore this day and turn your [mind and] heart to it that the Lord is God in the heavens above and upon the earth beneath; there is no other.

DEUTERONOMY 4:39 AMP

"But will God really dwell on earth? The heavens, even the highest heaven, cannot contain you. How much less this temple I have built!"

1 KINGS 8:27 NIV

The angel of the LORD encamps all around those who fear Him, and delivers them. Oh, taste and see that the LORD is good; blessed is the man who trusts in Him!

PSALM 34:7–8 NKJV

GOD is good, a hiding place in tough times. He recognizes and welcomes anyone looking for help, no matter how desperate the trouble.

NAHUM 1:7 MSG

"If we are not faithful, he will still be faithful. Christ cannot deny who he is."

2 TIMOTHY 2:13 CEV

Cast me not away from Your presence and take not Your Holy Spirit from me.

PSALM 51:11 AMP

Do you not know that your bodies are temples of the Holy Spirit, who is in you, whom you have received from God? You are not your own; you were bought at a price. Therefore honor God with your bodies.

1 CORINTHIANS 6:19–20 NIV

"Abide in Me, and I in you. As the branch cannot bear fruit of itself, unless it abides in the vine, neither can you, unless you abide in Me. I am the vine, you are the branches. He who abides in Me, and I in him, bears much fruit; for without Me you can do nothing."

JOHN 15:4–5 NKJV

Again Jesus said, "Peace be with you! As the Father
has sent me, I am sending you." And with that he
breathed on them and said, "Receive the Holy Spirit."

JOHN 20:21–22 NIV

"But the Helper, the Holy Spirit, whom the Father
will send in My name, He will teach you all things,
and bring to your remembrance all things that I said
to you."

JOHN 14:26 NKJV

"But you will receive power when the Holy Spirit
comes upon you. And you will be my witnesses,
telling people about me everywhere—in Jerusalem,
throughout Judea, in Samaria, and to the ends
of the earth."

ACTS 1:8 NLT

Meanwhile, the moment we get tired in the waiting,
God's Spirit is right alongside helping us along. If we
don't know how or what to pray, it doesn't matter.
He does our praying in and for us, making prayer out
of our wordless sighs, our aching groans. He knows
us far better than we know ourselves. . .and keeps us
present before God. That's why we can be so sure that
every detail in our lives of love for God is worked into
something good.

ROMANS 8:26–28 MSG

For I am persuaded beyond doubt (am sure) that neither death nor life, nor angels nor principalities, nor things impending and threatening nor things to come, nor powers, nor height nor depth, nor anything else in all creation will be able to separate us from the love of God which is in Christ Jesus our Lord.

ROMANS 8:38–39 AMP

As bad as you are, you still know how to give good gifts to your children. But your heavenly Father is even more ready to give the Holy Spirit to anyone who asks.

LUKE 11:13 CEV

What we have received is not the spirit of the world, but the Spirit who is from God, so that we may understand what God has freely given us.

1 CORINTHIANS 2:12 NIV

But the Holy Spirit produces this kind of fruit in our lives: love, joy, peace, patience, kindness, goodness, faithfulness.

GALATIANS 5:22 NLT

"The everlasting God is your place of safety, and his arms will hold you up forever. He will force your enemy out ahead of you, saying, 'Destroy the enemy!'"

DEUTERONOMY 33:27 NCV

"Am I a God who is only close at hand?" says the LORD. "No, I am far away at the same time. Can anyone hide from me in a secret place? Am I not everywhere in all the heavens and earth?" says the LORD.

JEREMIAH 23:23–24 NLT

Now hope does not disappoint, because the love of God has been poured out in our hearts by the Holy Spirit who was given to us.

ROMANS 5:5 NKJV

But you cannot make God accept you because of something you do. God accepts sinners only because they have faith in him.

ROMANS 4:5 CEV

But when the goodness and loving-kindness of God our Savior to man [as man] appeared, He saved us, not because of any works of righteousness that we had done, but because of His own pity and mercy, by [the] cleansing [bath] of the new birth (regeneration) and renewing of the Holy Spirit, Which He poured out [so] richly upon us through Jesus Christ our Savior.

TITUS 3:4–6 AMP

Christ came and preached peace to you outsiders and peace to us insiders. He treated us as equals, and so made us equals. Through him we both share the same Spirit and have equal access to the Father.

EPHESIANS 2:17–18 MSG

And the Lord said, My Presence shall go with you, and I will give you rest.

EXODUS 33:14 AMP

You will keep in perfect peace those whose minds are steadfast, because they trust in you. Trust in the LORD forever, for the LORD, the LORD himself, is the Rock eternal.

ISAIAH 26:3–4 NIV

He [God] Himself has said, I will not in any way fail you nor give you up nor leave you without support. [I will] not, [I will] not, [I will] not in any degree leave you helpless nor forsake nor let [you] down (relax My hold on you)! [Assuredly not!]

HEBREWS 13:5 AMP

God saved us from these great dangers of death, and he will continue to save us. We have put our hope in him, and he will save us again.

2 CORINTHIANS 1:10 NCV

The fundamental fact of existence is that this trust in God, this faith, is the firm foundation under everything that makes life worth living. It's our handle on what we can't see. The act of faith is what distinguished our ancestors, set them above the crowd.

HEBREWS 11:1–2 MSG

God Keeps
His Promises

Dear Lord, I have learned that people—even people who love me—will often let me down by failing to keep their promises. In those moments of disappointment, I sometimes need to be reminded that You are perfect and never go back on Your word. Help me to trust in Your promises, Lord. Give me the strength and courage to be more like You every day, so I can honor my promises to others. Amen.

And we know that all things work together for good to them that love God, to them who are the called according to his purpose.

ROMANS 8:28 KJV

Our LORD, let the heavens now praise your miracles, and let all of your angels praise your faithfulness.

PSALM 89:5 CEV

"Understand, therefore, that the LORD your God is indeed God. He is the faithful God who keeps his covenant for a thousand generations and lavishes his unfailing love on those who love him and obey his commands."

DEUTERONOMY 7:9 NLT

This truth gives them confidence that they have eternal life, which God—who does not lie— promised them before the world began.

TITUS 1:2 NLT

Who then is the faithful, thoughtful, and wise servant, whom his master has put in charge of his household to give to the others the food and supplies at the proper time? Blessed (happy, fortunate, and to be envied) is that servant whom, when his master comes, he will find so doing. I solemnly declare to you, he will set him over all his possessions.

MATTHEW 24:45–47 AMP

Because of these things, this is what the Lord GOD says: "I will put a stone in the ground in Jerusalem, a tested stone. Everything will be built on this important and precious rock. Anyone who trusts in it will never be disappointed."

ISAIAH 28:16 NCV

If we are unfaithful, he remains faithful, for he cannot deny who he is.

2 TIMOTHY 2:13 NLT

The Lord does not delay and is not tardy or slow about what He promises, according to some people's conception of slowness, but He is long-suffering (extraordinarily patient) toward you, not desiring that any should perish, but that all should turn to repentance.

2 PETER 3:9 AMP

For the LORD your God is a merciful God; he will not abandon or destroy you or forget the covenant with your ancestors, which he confirmed to them by oath.

DEUTERONOMY 4:31 NIV

Let us hold firmly to the hope that we have confessed, because we can trust God to do what he promised.

HEBREWS 10:23 NCV

"Remain faithful even when facing death, I will give you the crown of life."

REVELATION 2:10 NLT

Blessed be the Lord, Who has given rest to His people Israel, according to all that He promised. Not one word has failed of all His good promise which He promised through Moses His servant.

1 KINGS 8:56 AMP

"Have faith in me, and you will have life-giving water flowing from deep inside you, just as the Scriptures say."

JOHN 7:38 CEV

"Peace I leave with you, My peace I give to you; not as the world gives do I give to you. Let not your heart be troubled, neither let it be afraid."

JOHN 14:27 NKJV

Guide me in your truth, and teach me, my God, my Savior. I trust you all day long.

PSALM 25:5 NCV

During the meal, Jesus took and blessed the bread, broke it, and gave it to his disciples: Take, eat. This is my body. Taking the cup and thanking God, he gave it to them: Drink this, all of you. This is my blood, God's new covenant poured out for many people for the forgiveness of sins. "I'll not be drinking wine from this cup again until that new day when I'll drink with you in the kingdom of my Father."

MATTHEW 26:26–29 MSG

And Jesus said, [You say to Me], If You can do anything? [Why,] all things can be (are possible) to him who believes!

MARK 9:23 AMP

But Jesus said to them, "If you have faith and don't doubt, I promise that you can do what I did to this tree. And you will be able to do even more. You can tell this mountain to get up and jump into the sea, and it will. If you have faith when you pray, you will be given whatever you ask for."

MATTHEW 21:21–22 CEV

Your loyalty will go on and on; you made the earth, and it still stands.

PSALM 119:90 NCV

Like a will that takes effect when someone dies, the new covenant was put into action at Jesus' death. His death marked the transition from the old plan to the new one, canceling the old obligations and accompanying sins, and summoning the heirs to receive the eternal inheritance that was promised them. He brought together God and his people in this new way.

HEBREWS 9:16–17 MSG

And God said, This is the token of the covenant (solemn pledge) which I am making between Me and you and every living creature that is with you, for all future generations: I set My bow [rainbow] in the cloud, and it shall be a token or sign of a covenant or solemn pledge between Me and the earth. And it shall be that when I bring clouds over the earth and the bow [rainbow] is seen in the clouds, I will [earnestly] remember My covenant or solemn pledge which is between Me and you and every living creature of all flesh; and the waters will no more become a flood to destroy and make all flesh corrupt. When the bow [rainbow] is in the clouds and I look upon it, I will [earnestly] remember the everlasting covenant or pledge between God and every living creature of all flesh that is upon the earth. And God said to Noah, This [rainbow] is the token or sign of the covenant or solemn pledge which I have established between Me and all flesh upon the earth.

GENESIS 9:12–17 AMP

But the Lord is faithful, and he will strengthen you and protect you from the evil one.

2 THESSALONIANS 3:3 NIV

Commit your way to the LORD; trust in him and he will do this.

PSALM 37:5 NIV

But you cannot make God accept you because of something you do. God accepts sinners only because they have faith in him.

ROMANS 4:5 CEV

Love GOD, all you saints; GOD takes care of all who stay close to him, but he pays back in full those arrogant enough to go it alone.

PSALM 31:23 MSG

For the word of the LORD is right and true; he is faithful in all he does.

PSALM 33:4 NIV

The Lord also will be a refuge and a high tower for the oppressed, a refuge and a stronghold in times of trouble (high cost, destitution, and desperation). And they who know Your name [who have experience and acquaintance with Your mercy] will lean on and confidently put their trust in You, for You, Lord, have not forsaken those who seek (inquire of and for) You [on the authority of God's Word and the right of their necessity].

PSALM 9:9–10 AMP

Now may the God of peace, who through the blood of the eternal covenant brought back from the dead our Lord Jesus, that great Shepherd of the sheep, equip you with everything good for doing his will, and may he work in us what is pleasing to him, through Jesus Christ, to whom be glory for ever and ever. Amen.

HEBREWS 13:20–21 NIV

As you know, we count as blessed those who have persevered. You have heard of Job's perseverance and have seen what the Lord finally brought about. The Lord is full of compassion and mercy.

JAMES 5:11 NIV

"Today I have given you the choice between life and death, between blessings and curses. Now I call on heaven and earth to witness the choice you make. Oh, that you would choose life, so that you and your descendants might live! You can make this choice by loving the LORD your God, obeying him, and committing yourself firmly to him. This is the key to your life. And if you love and obey the LORD, you will live long in the land the LORD swore to give your ancestors Abraham, Isaac, and Jacob."

DEUTERONOMY 30:19–20 NLT

The instructions of the LORD are perfect, reviving the soul. The decrees of the LORD are trustworthy, making wise the simple.

PSALM 19:7 NLT

Does the Law disagree with God's promises? No, it doesn't! If any law could give life to us, we could become acceptable to God by obeying that law. But the Scriptures say that sin controls everyone, so that God's promises will be for anyone who has faith in Jesus Christ.

GALATIANS 3:21–22 CEV

They are the people of Israel, God's chosen children. They have seen the glory of God, and they have the agreements that God made between himself and his people. God gave them the law of Moses and the right way of worship and his promises.

ROMANS 9:4 NCV

This is because Jesus Christ the Son of God is always "Yes" and never "No." And he is the one that Silas, Timothy, and I told you about. Christ says "Yes" to all of God's promises. That's why we have Christ to say "Amen" for us to the glory of God. And so God makes it possible for you and us to stand firmly together with Christ. God is also the one who chose us.

2 CORINTHIANS 1:19–21 CEV

God
Knows Me

Heavenly Father, it's hard to imagine, but You know me better than my parents do! You know everything about me, even things that I don't know about myself—like how many hairs are on my head or how the rest of my life will turn out. Lord, I am blessed that You care so deeply for me. Thank You for loving me so much that You know every personal detail, even my quirks. Amen.

Nothing is hidden from God! He sees through everything, and we will have to tell him the truth.

HEBREWS 4:13 CEV

For your Father knows what you need before you ask Him.

MATTHEW 6:8 AMP

"So go and make followers of all people in the world. Baptize them in the name of the Father and the Son and the Holy Spirit. Teach them to obey everything that I have taught you, and I will be with you always, even until the end of this age."

MATTHEW 28:19–20 NCV

GOD, my shepherd! I don't need a thing. You have bedded me down in lush meadows, you find me quiet pools to drink from. True to your word, you let me catch my breath and send me in the right direction. Even when the way goes through Death Valley, I'm not afraid when you walk at my side. Your trusty shepherd's crook makes me feel secure.

PSALM 23:1–4 MSG

The LORD thy God in the midst of thee is mighty; he will save, he will rejoice over thee with joy; he will rest in his love, he will joy over thee with singing.

ZEPHANIAH 3:17 KJV

He determines the number of the stars and calls them each by name.

PSALM 147:4 NIV

Nothing and no one is holy like GOD, no rock mountain like our God. Don't dare talk pretentiously—not a word of boasting, ever! For GOD knows what's going on. He takes the measure of everything that happens.

1 SAMUEL 2:2–3 MSG

Just think—you don't need a thing, you've got it all! All God's gifts are right in front of you as you wait expectantly for our Master Jesus to arrive on the scene for the Finale. And not only that, but God himself is right alongside to keep you steady and on track until things are all wrapped up by Jesus. God, who got you started in this spiritual adventure, shares with us the life of his Son and our Master Jesus. He will never give up on you. Never forget that.

1 CORINTHIANS 1:7–9 MSG

"I always see the Lord near me, and I will not be afraid with him at my right side. Because of this, my heart will be glad, my words will be joyful, and I will live in hope. The Lord won't leave me in the grave. I am his holy one, and he won't let my body decay."

ACTS 2:25–27 CEV

Yes, God's riches are very great, and his wisdom and knowledge have no end! No one can explain the things God decides or understand his ways.

ROMANS 11:33 NCV

"Even the very hairs of your head are all numbered."

MATTHEW 10:30 NIV

"Understand, therefore, that the LORD your God is indeed God. He is the faithful God who keeps his covenant for a thousand generations and lavishes his unfailing love on those who love him and obey his commands."

DEUTERONOMY 7:9 NLT

He knows us far better than we know ourselves. . . and keeps us present before God. That's why we can be so sure that every detail in our lives of love for God is worked into something good.

ROMANS 8:28 MSG

And if anyone thinks that he knows anything, he knows nothing yet as he ought to know. But if anyone loves God, this one is known by Him.

1 CORINTHIANS 8:2–3 NKJV

This resurrection life you received from God is not a timid, grave-tending life. It's adventurously expectant, greeting God with a childlike "What's next, Papa?" God's Spirit touches our spirits and confirms who we really are. We know who he is, and we know who we are: Father and children. And we know we are going to get what's coming to us—an unbelievable inheritance! We go through exactly what Christ goes through. If we go through the hard times with him, then we're certainly going to go through the good times with him!

ROMANS 8:15–17 MSG

Also, the Spirit helps us with our weakness. We do not know how to pray as we should. But the Spirit himself speaks to God for us, even begs God for us with deep feelings that words cannot explain.

ROMANS 8:26 NCV

Search me, God, and know my heart; test me and know my anxious thoughts. See if there is any offensive way in me, and lead me in the way everlasting.

PSALM 139:23–24 NIV

"Eye has not seen, nor ear heard, nor have entered into the heart of man the things which God has prepared for those who love Him."

1 CORINTHIANS 2:9 NKJV

"Accept the God of your father. Serve him completely and willingly, because the LORD knows what is in everyone's mind. He understands everything you think. If you go to him for help, you will get an answer."

1 CHRONICLES 28:9 NCV

The Lord looks from heaven, He beholds all the sons of men; from His dwelling place He looks [intently] upon all the inhabitants of the earth—He Who fashions the hearts of them all, Who considers all their doings.

PSALM 33:13–15 AMP

No, God has not rejected his own people, whom he chose from the very beginning.

ROMANS 11:2 NLT

Praise be to the God and Father of our Lord Jesus Christ, the Father of compassion and the God of all comfort, who comforts us in all our troubles, so that we can comfort those in any trouble with the comfort we ourselves receive from God. For just as we share abundantly in the sufferings of Christ, so also our comfort abounds through Christ.

2 CORINTHIANS 1:3–5 NIV

Before you knew God, you were slaves of gods that are not real. But now you know God, or better still, God knows you.

GALATIANS 4:8–9 CEV

But the LORD said to Samuel, "Don't judge by his appearance or height, for I have rejected him. The LORD doesn't see things the way you see them. People judge by outward appearance, but the LORD looks at the heart."

1 SAMUEL 16:7 NLT

God our Father loves us. He is kind and has given us eternal comfort and a wonderful hope. We pray that our Lord Jesus Christ and God our Father will encourage you and help you always to do and say the right thing.

2 THESSALONIANS 2:16–17 CEV

But even there, if you seek GOD, your God, you'll be able to find him if you're serious, looking for him with your whole heart and soul. When troubles come and all these awful things happen to you, in future days you will come back to GOD, your God, and listen obediently to what he says. GOD, your God, is above all a compassionate God. In the end he will not abandon you, he won't bring you to ruin, he won't forget the covenant with your ancestors which he swore to them.

DEUTERONOMY 4:29–31 MSG

God Loves Me

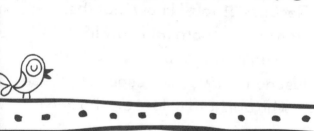

Dear Lord, Your ability to love is nothing short of amazing. You love with a sacrificial love that does not come naturally to me. You even sent Your own Son to die for a world that wasn't deserving of Your love! Because of You, I know that there will never be a moment in my life that I am unloved. Help me to love others just as You love me—especially those who are hard to love or who don't love me back. Amen.

God stays one with everyone who openly says that Jesus is the Son of God. That's how we stay one with God and are sure that God loves us. God is love. If we keep on loving others, we will stay one in our hearts with God, and he will stay one with us.

1 JOHN 4:15–16 CEV

This is real love—not that we loved God, but that he loved us and sent his Son as a sacrifice to take away our sins.

1 JOHN 4:10 NLT

GOD sticks by all who love him, but it's all over for those who don't.

PSALM 145:20 MSG

God loved the people of this world so much that he gave his only Son, so that everyone who has faith in him will have eternal life and never really die.

JOHN 3:16 CEV

We can understand someone dying for a person worth dying for, and we can understand how someone good and noble could inspire us to selfless sacrifice. But God put his love on the line for us by offering his Son in sacrificial death while we were of no use whatever to him.

ROMANS 5:7–8 MSG

Think how much the Father loves us. He loves us so much that he lets us be called his children, as we truly are.

1 JOHN 3:1 CEV

This is how God showed his love to us: He sent his one and only Son into the world so that we could have life through him.

1 JOHN 4:9 NCV

"I will heal their waywardness and love them freely, for my anger has turned away from them."

HOSEA 14:4 NIV

That is what the Scriptures mean when they say, "No eye has seen, no ear has heard, and no mind has imagined what God has prepared for those who love him."

1 CORINTHIANS 2:9 NLT

For I am persuaded beyond doubt (am sure) that neither death nor life, nor angels nor principalities, nor things impending and threatening nor things to come, nor powers, nor height nor depth, nor anything else in all creation will be able to separate us from the love of God which is in Christ Jesus our Lord.

ROMANS 8:38–39 AMP

"I've told you these things for a purpose: that my joy might be your joy, and your joy wholly mature. This is my command: Love one another the way I loved you. This is the very best way to love. Put your life on the line for your friends. You are my friends when you do the things I command you."

JOHN 15:11–13 MSG

Clothe yourselves therefore, as God's own chosen ones (His own picked representatives), [who are] purified and holy and well-beloved [by God Himself, by putting on behavior marked by] tenderhearted pity and mercy, kind feeling, a lowly opinion of yourselves, gentle ways, [and] patience [which is tireless and long-suffering, and has the power to endure whatever comes, with good temper].

COLOSSIANS 3:12 AMP

We have confidence in the Lord that you are doing and will continue to do the things we command. May the Lord direct your hearts into God's love and Christ's perseverance.

2 THESSALONIANS 3:4–5 NIV

"For the LORD your God is living among you. He is a mighty savior. He will take delight in you with gladness. With his love, he will calm all your fears. He will rejoice over you with joyful songs."

ZEPHANIAH 3:17 NLT

"But let him who glories glory in this, that he understands and knows Me, that I am the LORD, exercising lovingkindness, judgment, and righteousness in the earth. For in these I delight," says the LORD.

JEREMIAH 9:24 NKJV

My whole being, praise the LORD and do not forget all his kindnesses. He forgives all my sins and heals all my diseases. He saves my life from the grave and loads me with love and mercy.

PSALM 103:2–4 NCV

Long ago the LORD said to Israel: "I have loved you, my people, with an everlasting love. With unfailing love I have drawn you to myself."

JEREMIAH 31:3 NLT

Examine me, O Lord, and prove me; test my heart and my mind. For Your loving-kindness is before my eyes, and I have walked in Your truth [faithfully].

PSALM 26:2–3 AMP

How exquisite your love, O God! How eager we are to run under your wings, to eat our fill at the banquet you spread as you fill our tankards with Eden spring water. You're a fountain of cascading light, and you open our eyes to light.

PSALM 36:7–9 MSG

Then the LORD came down in the cloud and stood there with him and proclaimed his name, the LORD. And he passed in front of Moses, proclaiming, "The LORD, the LORD, the compassionate and gracious God, slow to anger, abounding in love and faithfulness, maintaining love to thousands, and forgiving wickedness, rebellion and sin."

EXODUS 34:5–7 NIV

"I have loved you," says the LORD.

MALACHI 1:2 NIV

Understand, therefore, that the LORD your God is indeed God. He is the faithful God who keeps his covenant for a thousand generations and lavishes his unfailing love on those who love him and obey his commands.

DEUTERONOMY 7:9 NLT

Thank GOD! He deserves your thanks. His love never quits. Thank the God of all gods, His love never quits. Thank the Lord of all lords. His love never quits.

PSALM 136:1–3 MSG

But I am like an olive tree growing in God's house, and I can count on his love forever and ever.

PSALM 52:8 CEV

Let us then fearlessly and confidently and boldly draw near to the throne of grace (the throne of God's unmerited favor to us sinners), that we may receive mercy [for our failures] and find grace to help in good time for every need [appropriate help and well-timed help, coming just when we need it].

HEBREWS 4:16 AMP

My God is my rock, in whom I find protection. He is my shield, the power that saves me, and my place of safety. He is my refuge, my savior, the one who saves me from violence.

2 SAMUEL 22:3 NLT

I love those who love me, and those who seek me diligently will find me.

PROVERBS 8:17 NKJV

Have mercy on me, O God, according to your unfailing love; according to your great compassion blot out my transgressions. Wash away all my iniquity and cleanse me from my sin. For I know my transgressions, and my sin is always before me. Against you, you only, have I sinned and done what is evil in your sight; so you are right in your verdict and justified when you judge.

PSALM 51:1–4 NIV

God loves you and has chosen you to be his very own people.

ROMANS 1:7 CEV

"Whoever has my commands and keeps them is the one who loves me. The one who loves me will be loved by my Father, and I too will love them and show myself to them."

JOHN 14:21 NIV

"This is how much God loved the world: He gave his Son, his one and only Son. And this is why: so that no one need be destroyed; by believing in him, anyone can have a whole and lasting life. God didn't go to all the trouble of sending his Son merely to point an accusing finger, telling the world how bad it was. He came to help, to put the world right again."

JOHN 3:16–17 MSG

But I trust in your unfailing love. I will rejoice because you have rescued me.

PSALM 13:5 NLT

"As the Father loved Me, I also have loved you; abide in My love. If you keep My commandments, you will abide in My love, just as I have kept My Father's commandments and abide in His love."

JOHN 15:9–10 NKJV

Now about your love for one another we do not need to write to you, for you yourselves have been taught by God to love each other.

1 THESSALONIANS 4:9 NIV

"A new commandment I give to you, that you love one another; as I have loved you, that you also love one another. By this all will know that you are My disciples, if you have love for one another."

JOHN 13:34–35 NKJV

"The Father himself loves you. He loves you because you loved me and believed that I came from God."

JOHN 16:27 NCV

But God shows and clearly proves His [own] love for us by the fact that while we were still sinners, Christ (the Messiah, the Anointed One) died for us.

ROMANS 5:8 AMP

"The God who made the world and everything in it is the Lord of heaven and earth and does not live in temples built by human hands. And he is not served by human hands, as if he needed anything. Rather, he himself gives everyone life and breath and everything else. From one man he made all the nations, that they should inhabit the whole earth; and he marked out their appointed times in history and the boundaries of their lands. God did this so that they would seek him and perhaps reach out for him and find him, though he is not far from any one of us."

ACTS 17:24–27 NIV

God Made Me

Dear God, You thought of me and planned my existence, even before You created the entire world! Everything about me—from how I look, to my personality and preferences, to my abilities—was created by You and should glorify You, Lord. When I criticize or want to change something about myself, please help me to remember the care that You took to make me. Also, help me to remember that after You were finished with all of Your creation, You said it was good. Please give me the ability to have the same positive attitude when I look at the world around me. Amen.

You made all the delicate, inner parts of my body
and knit me together in my mother's womb.

PSALM 139:13 NLT

Then God said, "Let us make human beings in our
image and likeness. And let them rule over the fish
in the sea and the birds in the sky, over the tame
animals, over all the earth, and over all the small
crawling animals on the earth." So God created
human beings in his image. In the image of God he
created them. He created them male and female.
God blessed them and said, "Have many children
and grow in number. Fill the earth and be its master.
Rule over the fish in the sea and over the birds in
the sky and over every living thing that moves on
the earth."

GENESIS 1:26–28 NCV

And God saw everything that He had made, and
behold, it was very good (suitable, pleasant) and He
approved it completely. And there was evening and
there was morning, a sixth day.

GENESIS 1:31 AMP

Even before he made the world, God loved us and
chose us in Christ to be holy and without fault in
his eyes.

EPHESIANS 1:4 NLT

"The God who made the world and everything in it is the Lord of heaven and earth and does not live in temples built by human hands. And he is not served by human hands, as if he needed anything. Rather, he himself gives everyone life and breath and everything else. From one man he made all the nations, that they should inhabit the whole earth; and he marked out their appointed times in history and the boundaries of their lands. God did this so that they would seek him and perhaps reach out for him and find him, though he is not far from any one of us."

ACTS 17:24–27 NIV

Still, GOD, you are our Father. We're the clay and you're our potter: All of us are what you made us. Don't be too angry with us, O GOD.

ISAIAH 64:8 MSG

Many are the plans in a person's heart, but it is the LORD's purpose that prevails.

PROVERBS 19:21 NIV

"For I know the plans I have for you," says the LORD. "They are plans for good and not for disaster, to give you a future and a hope."

JEREMIAH 29:11 NLT

See what [an incredible] quality of love the Father has given (shown, bestowed on) us, that we should [be permitted to] be named and called and counted the children of God! And so we are! The reason that the world does not know (recognize, acknowledge) us is that it does not know (recognize, acknowledge) Him.

1 JOHN 3:1 AMP

Come, let us worship and bow down. Let us kneel before the LORD our maker.

PSALM 95:6 NLT

You made me and formed me with your hands. Give me understanding so I can learn your commands.

PSALM 119:73 NCV

Your hands have formed me and made me. Would You turn around and destroy me? Remember [earnestly], I beseech You, that You have fashioned me as clay [out of the same earth material, exquisitely and elaborately]. And will You bring me into dust again? Have You not poured me out like milk and curdled me like cheese? You have clothed me with skin and flesh and have knit me together with bones and sinews. You have granted me life and favor, and Your providence has preserved my spirit.

JOB 10:8–12 AMP

The LORD will perfect that which concerns me; Your mercy, O LORD, endures forever; do not forsake the works of Your hands.

PSALM 138:8 NKJV

Now God has us where he wants us, with all the time in this world and the next to shower grace and kindness upon us in Christ Jesus. Saving is all his idea, and all his work. All we do is trust him enough to let him do it. It's God's gift from start to finish! We don't play the major role. If we did, we'd probably go around bragging that we'd done the whole thing! No, we neither make nor save ourselves. God does both the making and saving. He creates each of us by Christ Jesus to join him in the work he does, the good work he has gotten ready for us to do, work we had better be doing.

EPHESIANS 2:7–10 MSG

You are the one who put me together inside my mother's body, and I praise you because of the wonderful way you created me. Everything you do is marvelous! Of this I have no doubt. Nothing about me is hidden from you! I was secretly woven together deep in the earth below, but with your own eyes you saw my body being formed. Even before I was born, you had written in your book everything I would do.

PSALM 139:13–16 CEV

"Remain in me, as I also remain in you. No branch can bear fruit by itself; it must remain in the vine. Neither can you bear fruit unless you remain in me. I am the vine; you are the branches. If you remain in me and I in you, you will bear much fruit; apart from me you can do nothing."

JOHN 15:4–5 NIV

I have written to you who are God's children because you know the Father. I have written to you who are mature in the faith because you know Christ, who existed from the beginning. I have written to you who are young in the faith because you are strong. God's word lives in your hearts, and you have won your battle with the evil one.

1 JOHN 2:14 NLT

Do you not know that your bodies are temples of the Holy Spirit, who is in you, whom you have received from God? You are not your own; you were bought at a price. Therefore honor God with your bodies.

1 CORINTHIANS 6:19–20 NIV

"Before I shaped you in the womb, I knew all about you. Before you saw the light of day, I had holy plans for you: A prophet to the nations—that's what I had in mind for you."

JEREMIAH 1:5 MSG

From high in the skies GOD looks around, he sees all Adam's brood. From where he sits he overlooks all us earth-dwellers. He has shaped each person in turn; now he watches everything we do.

PSALM 33:13–15 MSG

Shout to the LORD, all the earth. Serve the LORD with joy; come before him with singing. Know that the LORD is God. He made us, and we belong to him; we are his people, the sheep he tends. Come into his city with songs of thanksgiving and into his courtyards with songs of praise. Thank him and praise his name. The LORD is good. His love is forever, and his loyalty goes on and on.

PSALM 100 NCV

And we have known and believed the love that God has for us. God is love, and he who abides in love abides in God, and God in him.

1 JOHN 4:16 NKJV

God
Offers Me
Eternal Life

Dear God, it's so easy to get distracted by my life here on earth, and I sometimes forget that this is not the only life I will have. You have promised eternal life in heaven with You to all who accept it—through Jesus' death on the cross, which made my salvation possible. Help me to think often of my eternal life yet to come— a life free from worry, sadness, and sin. Thank You, Father. Amen.

"Those who love their lives will lose them, but those who hate their lives in this world will keep true life forever."

JOHN 12:25 NCV

Sin pays off with death. But God's gift is eternal life given by Jesus Christ our Lord.

ROMANS 6:23 CEV

For we know that if the earthly tent we live in is destroyed, we have a building from God, an eternal house in heaven, not built by human hands.

2 CORINTHIANS 5:1 NIV

But let me reveal to you a wonderful secret. We will not all die, but we will all be transformed! It will happen in a moment, in the blink of an eye, when the last trumpet is blown. For when the trumpet sounds, those who have died will be raised to live forever. And we who are living will also be transformed. For our dying bodies must be transformed into bodies that will never die; our mortal bodies must be transformed into immortal bodies. Then, when our dying bodies have been transformed into bodies that will never die, this Scripture will be fulfilled: "Death is swallowed up in victory."

1 CORINTHIANS 15:51–54 NLT

In my Father's house are many mansions: if it were not so, I would have told you. I go to prepare a place for you. And if I go and prepare a place for you, I will come again, and receive you unto myself; that where I am, there ye may be also.

JOHN 14:2–3 KJV

And now the prize awaits me—the crown of righteousness, which the Lord, the righteous Judge, will give me on the day of his return. And the prize is not just for me but for all who eagerly look forward to his appearing.

2 TIMOTHY 4:8 NLT

Then I saw "a new heaven and a new earth," for the first heaven and the first earth had passed away, and there was no longer any sea. I saw the Holy City, the new Jerusalem, coming down out of heaven from God, prepared as a bride beautifully dressed for her husband.

REVELATION 21:1–2 NIV

Jesus said, "Come to think of it, you are going to drink my cup. But as to awarding places of honor, that's not my business. My Father is taking care of that."

MATTHEW 20:23 MSG

There will be no more night. They will not need the light of a lamp or the light of the sun, for the Lord God will give them light. And they will reign for ever and ever.

REVELATION 22:5 NIV

I tell you for certain that everyone who hears my message and has faith in the one who sent me has eternal life and will never be condemned. They have already gone from death to life.

JOHN 5:24 CEV

The world and everything that people want in it are passing away, but the person who does what God wants lives forever.

1 JOHN 2:17 NCV

Praised (honored, blessed) be the God and Father of our Lord Jesus Christ (the Messiah)! By His boundless mercy we have been born again to an ever-living hope through the resurrection of Jesus Christ from the dead, [born anew] into an inheritance which is beyond the reach of change and decay [imperishable], unsullied and unfading, reserved in heaven for you, who are being guarded (garrisoned) by God's power through [your] faith [till you fully inherit that final] salvation that is ready to be revealed [for you] in the last time.

1 PETER 1:3–5 AMP

Jesus then said, "I am the one who raises the dead to life! Everyone who has faith in me will live, even if they die. And everyone who lives because of faith in me will never really die. Do you believe this?"

JOHN 11:25–26 CEV

But because you are stubborn and refuse to turn from your sin, you are storing up terrible punishment for yourself. For a day of anger is coming, when God's righteous judgment will be revealed. He will judge everyone according to what they have done. He will give eternal life to those who keep on doing good, seeking after the glory and honor and immortality that God offers.

ROMANS 2:5–7 NLT

"Don't work for the food that spoils. Work for the food that stays good always and gives eternal life. The Son of Man will give you this food, because on him God the Father has put his power."

JOHN 6:27 NCV

But if the Spirit of Him who raised Jesus from the dead dwells in you, He who raised Christ from the dead will also give life to your mortal bodies through His Spirit who dwells in you.

ROMANS 8:11 NKJV

Since everything here today might well be gone tomorrow, do you see how essential it is to live a holy life? Daily expect the Day of God, eager for its arrival. The galaxies will burn up and the elements melt down that day—but we'll hardly notice. We'll be looking the other way, ready for the promised new heavens and the promised new earth, all landscaped with righteousness.

2 PETER 3:11–13 MSG

Those who live only to satisfy their own sinful nature will harvest decay and death from that sinful nature. But those who live to please the Spirit will harvest everlasting life from the Spirit.

GALATIANS 6:8 NLT

Then when Christ the Chief Shepherd returns, you will be given a crown that will never lose its glory.

1 PETER 5:4 CEV

And many of them that sleep in the dust of the earth shall awake, some to everlasting life, and some to shame and everlasting contempt.

DANIEL 12:2 KJV

Jesus answered, "Everyone who drinks this water will be thirsty again, but whoever drinks the water I give them will never thirst. Indeed, the water I give them will become in them a spring of water welling up to eternal life."

JOHN 4:13–14 NIV

He has made everything beautiful in its time. He also has planted eternity in men's hearts and minds [a divinely implanted sense of a purpose working through the ages which nothing under the sun but God alone can satisfy], yet so that men cannot find out what God has done from the beginning to the end.

ECCLESIASTES 3:11 AMP

But I was given mercy so that in me, the worst of all sinners, Christ Jesus could show that he has patience without limit. His patience with me made me an example for those who would believe in him and have life forever. To the King that rules forever, who will never die, who cannot be seen, the only God, be honor and glory forever and ever. Amen.

1 TIMOTHY 1:16–17 NCV

My Father wants everyone who sees the Son to have faith in him and to have eternal life. Then I will raise them to life on the last day.

JOHN 6:40 CEV

"Those who believe in the Son have eternal life, but those who do not obey the Son will never have life. God's anger stays on them."

JOHN 3:36 NCV

But now that you've found you don't have to listen to sin tell you what to do, and have discovered the delight of listening to God telling you, what a surprise! A whole, healed, put-together life right now, with more and more of life on the way! Work hard for sin your whole life and your pension is death. But God's gift is real life, eternal life, delivered by Jesus, our Master.

ROMANS 6:22–23 MSG

"For you have given him authority over everyone. He gives eternal life to each one you have given him. And this is the way to have eternal life—to know you, the only true God, and Jesus Christ, the one you sent to earth."

JOHN 17:2–3 NLT

Now behold, one came and said to Him, "Good Teacher, what good thing shall I do that I may have eternal life?" So He said to him, "Why do you call Me good? No one is good but One, that is, God. But if you want to enter into life, keep the commandments."

MATTHEW 19:16–17 NKJV

"For God loved the world so much that he gave his one and only Son, so that everyone who believes in him will not perish but have eternal life."

JOHN 3:16 NLT

"Therefore they are before the throne of God, and serve Him day and night in His temple. And He who sits on the throne will dwell among them. They shall neither hunger anymore nor thirst anymore; the sun shall not strike them, nor any heat; for the Lamb who is in the midst of the throne will shepherd them and lead them to living fountains of waters. And God will wipe away every tear from their eyes."

REVELATION 7:15–17 NKJV

And I give unto them eternal life; and they shall never perish, neither shall any man pluck them out of my hand.

JOHN 10:28 KJV

"You carefully study the Scriptures because you think they give you eternal life. They do in fact tell about me."

JOHN 5:39 NCV

So just as sin ruled over all people and brought them to death, now God's wonderful grace rules instead, giving us right standing with God and resulting in eternal life through Jesus Christ our Lord.

ROMANS 5:21 NLT

God
Protects Me

Dear Lord, not only do You never leave me or forsake me, but You always protect and shelter me in the palm of Your hand. You send Your angels to surround me. Nothing can separate me from Your protection. Although I do not fully understand Your protection, Lord, I trust it is there. Remind me of Your power whenever I doubt, Lord, and help me to feel safe and secure in You, no matter what happens in my life. Amen.

Surely, LORD, you bless the righteous; you surround them with your favor as with a shield.

PSALM 5:12 NIV

"The LORD lives! Blessed be my Rock! Let God be exalted, the Rock of my salvation!"

2 SAMUEL 22:47 NKJV

You have given me your shield of victory. Your right hand supports me; your help has made me great.

PSALM 18:35 NLT

The LORD is a mighty tower where his people can run for safety.

PROVERBS 18:10 CEV

We wait in hope for the LORD; he is our help and our shield.

PSALM 33:20 NIV

Every word of God is pure: he is a shield unto them that put their trust in him.

PROVERBS 30:5 KJV

He will cover you with his feathers, and under his wings you can hide. His truth will be your shield and protection.

PSALM 91:4 NCV

"When you go through deep waters, I will be with you. When you go through rivers of difficulty, you will not drown. When you walk through the fire of oppression, you will not be burned up; the flames will not consume you."

ISAIAH 43:2 NLT

Be my mighty rock, the place where I can always run for protection. Save me by your command! You are my mighty rock and my fortress.

PSALM 71:3 CEV

But the LORD is my fortress; my God is the mighty rock where I hide.

PSALM 94:22 NLT

Be prepared. You're up against far more than you can handle on your own. Take all the help you can get, every weapon God has issued, so that when it's all over but the shouting you'll still be on your feet. Truth, righteousness, peace, faith, and salvation are more than words. Learn how to apply them. You'll need them throughout your life. God's Word is an indispensable weapon. In the same way, prayer is essential in this ongoing warfare. Pray hard and long. Pray for your brothers and sisters. Keep your eyes open. Keep each other's spirits up so that no one falls behind or drops out.

EPHESIANS 6:13–18 MSG

He said: The Lord is my Rock [of escape from Saul] and my Fortress [in the wilderness] and my Deliverer; My God, my Rock, in Him will I take refuge; my Shield and the Horn of my salvation; my Stronghold and my Refuge, my Savior—You save me from violence. I call on the Lord, Who is worthy to be praised, and I am saved from my enemies.

2 SAMUEL 22:2–4 AMP

The LORD is good. He protects those who trust him in times of trouble.

NAHUM 1:7 CEV

God is our Refuge and Strength [mighty and impenetrable to temptation], a very present and well-proved help in trouble. Therefore we will not fear, though the earth should change and though the mountains be shaken into the midst of the seas, though its waters roar and foam, though the mountains tremble at its swelling and tumult. Selah [pause, and calmly think of that]!

PSALM 46:1–3 AMP

The eternal God is thy refuge, and underneath are the everlasting arms.

DEUTERONOMY 33:27 KJV

The LORD is a shelter for the oppressed, a refuge in times of trouble.

PSALM 9:9 NLT

The LORD Most High is your fortress. Run to him for safety, and no terrible disasters will strike you or your home. God will command his angels to protect you wherever you go. They will carry you in their arms, and you won't hurt your feet on the stones.

PSALM 91:9–12 CEV

I have told you this, so that you might have peace in your hearts because of me. While you are in the world, you will have to suffer. But cheer up! I have defeated the world.

JOHN 16:33 CEV

Many are the afflictions of the righteous: but the LORD delivereth him out of them all.

PSALM 34:19 KJV

Your kingdom is an everlasting kingdom, and your dominion endures through all generations. The LORD is trustworthy in all he promises and faithful in all he does. The LORD upholds all who fall and lifts up all who are bowed down. The eyes of all look to you, and you give them their food at the proper time. You open your hand and satisfy the desires of every living thing.

PSALM 145:13–16 NIV

Rejoice not against me, O my enemy! When I fall, I shall arise; when I sit in darkness, the Lord shall be a light to me. I will bear the indignation of the Lord because I have sinned against Him, until He pleads my cause and executes judgment for me. He will bring me forth to the light, and I shall behold His righteous deliverance.

MICAH 7:8–9 AMP

So the king gave the order, and they brought Daniel and threw him into the lions' den. The king said to Daniel, "May your God, whom you serve continually, rescue you!" A stone was brought and placed over the mouth of the den, and the king sealed it with his own signet ring and with the rings of his nobles, so that Daniel's situation might not be changed. . . . At the first light of dawn, the king got up and hurried to the lions' den. When he came near the den, he called to Daniel in an anguished voice, "Daniel, servant of the living God, has your God, whom you serve continually, been able to rescue you from the lions?" Daniel answered, "May the king live forever! My God sent his angel, and he shut the mouths of the lions. They have not hurt me, because I was found innocent in his sight."

DANIEL 6:16–17, 19–22 NIV

Behold, the Lord God will come with might, and His arm will rule for Him. Behold, His reward is with Him, and His recompense before Him.

ISAIAH 40:10 AMP

"Do not be afraid. For I have bought you and made you free. I have called you by name. You are Mine!"

ISAIAH 43:1 NLV

Jesus looked at them and said, "With man this is impossible, but with God all things are possible."

MATTHEW 19:26 NIV

The LORD All-Powerful is with us; the God of Jacob is our defender. Selah

PSALM 46:7 NCV

"Yours, LORD, is the greatness and the power and the glory and the majesty and the splendor, for everything in heaven and earth is yours. Yours, LORD, is the kingdom; you are exalted as head over all. Wealth and honor come from you; you are the ruler of all things. In your hands are strength and power to exalt and give strength to all."

1 CHRONICLES 29:11–12 NIV

In the fear of the LORD is strong confidence: and his children shall have a place of refuge.

PROVERBS 14:26 KJV

Cast your burden on the LORD, and He shall sustain you; He shall never permit the righteous to be moved.

PSALM 55:22 NKJV

God Thinks
I'm Beautiful

Heavenly Father, most of the time I don't feel all that beautiful. I evaluate my looks with a critical eye. And I often compare myself to other girls and find myself wishing I were more like them. Lord, help me to see myself—and others—through Your eyes. You designed us just as we are, and You think we're beautiful! Thank You, Father. Help me to be beautiful on the inside and to find contentment just as I am on the outside—Your unique and lovely creation. Amen.

Don't copy the behavior and customs of this world, but let God transform you into a new person by changing the way you think. Then you will learn to know God's will for you, which is good and pleasing and perfect.

Romans 12:2 NLT

I want women to get in there with the men in humility before God, not primping before a mirror or chasing the latest fashions but doing something beautiful for God and becoming beautiful doing it.

1 Timothy 2:9–10 MSG

It's healthy to be content, but envy can eat you up.

Proverbs 14:30 CEV

Lean on, trust in, and be confident in the Lord with all your heart and mind and do not rely on your own insight or understanding. In all your ways know, recognize, and acknowledge Him, and He will direct and make straight and plain your paths.

Proverbs 3:5–6 AMP

Give your worries to the LORD, and he will take care of you. He will never let good people down.

Psalm 55:22 NCV

"The LORD doesn't see things the way you see them. People judge by outward appearance, but the LORD looks at the heart."

1 Samuel 16:7 NLT

Anyone who belongs to Christ has become a new person. The old life is gone; a new life has begun!

2 CORINTHIANS 5:17 NLT

Let us not become vainglorious and self-conceited, competitive and challenging and provoking and irritating to one another, envying and being jealous of one another.

GALATIANS 5:26 AMP

Be honest in your judgment and do not decide at a glance (superficially and by appearances); but judge fairly and righteously.

JOHN 7:24 AMP

Charm can be deceiving, and beauty fades away, but a woman who honors the LORD deserves to be praised.

PROVERBS 31:30 CEV

Your beauty should not come from outward adornment, such as elaborate hairstyles and the wearing of gold jewelry or fine clothes. Rather, it should be that of your inner self, the unfading beauty of a gentle and quiet spirit, which is of great worth in God's sight. For this is the way the holy women of the past who put their hope in God used to adorn themselves.

1 PETER 3:3–5 NIV

Listen, daughter, and pay careful attention: Forget your people and your father's house. Let the king be enthralled by your beauty; honor him, for he is your lord.

PSALM 45:10–11 NIV

So God created man in His own image, in the image and likeness of God He created him; male and female He created them.

GENESIS 1:27 AMP

You, LORD, are our Father. We are nothing but clay, but you are the potter who molded us.

ISAIAH 64:8 CEV

Delight yourself also in the Lord, and He will give you the desires and secret petitions of your heart.

PSALM 37:4 AMP

People who are ruled by their desires think only of themselves. Everyone who is ruled by the Holy Spirit thinks about spiritual things.

ROMANS 8:5 CEV

Let love be your highest goal! But you should also desire the special abilities the Spirit gives.

1 CORINTHIANS 14:1 NLT

Just as He chose us in Him before the foundation of the world, that we should be holy and without blame before Him in love.

EPHESIANS 1:4 NKJV

But make sure that you don't get so absorbed and exhausted in taking care of all your day-by-day obligations that you lose track of the time and doze off, oblivious to God. The night is about over, dawn is about to break. Be up and awake to what God is doing! God is putting the finishing touches on the salvation work he began when we first believed. We can't afford to waste a minute, must not squander these precious daylight hours in frivolity and indulgence, in sleeping around and dissipation, in bickering and grabbing everything in sight. Get out of bed and get dressed! Don't loiter and linger, waiting until the very last minute. Dress yourselves in Christ, and be up and about!

ROMANS 13:11–14 MSG

Finally, brethren, whatever things are true, whatever things are noble, whatever things are just, whatever things are pure, whatever things are lovely, whatever things are of good report, if there is any virtue and if there is anything praiseworthy— meditate on these things.

PHILIPPIANS 4:8 NKJV

For we are God's masterpiece. He has created us anew in Christ Jesus, so we can do the good things he planned for us long ago.

EPHESIANS 2:10 NLT

"The LORD will guide you always; he will satisfy your needs in a sun-scorched land and will strengthen your frame. You will be like a well-watered garden, like a spring whose waters never fail."

ISAIAH 58:11 NIV

See how very much our Father loves us, for he calls us his children, and that is what we are! But the people who belong to this world don't recognize that we are God's children because they don't know him.

1 JOHN 3:1 NLT

Her clothes are well-made and elegant, and she always faces tomorrow with a smile. When she speaks she has something worthwhile to say, and she always says it kindly.

PROVERBS 31:25–26 MSG

These people think religion is supposed to make you rich. And religion does make your life rich, by making you content with what you have. We didn't bring anything into this world, and we won't take anything with us when we leave.

1 TIMOTHY 6:5–7 CEV

Do you not know that your bodies are temples of the Holy Spirit, who is in you, whom you have received from God? You are not your own; you were bought at a price. Therefore honor God with your bodies.

1 CORINTHIANS 6:19–20 NIV

Do not let all kinds of strange teachings lead you into the wrong way. Your hearts should be strengthened by God's grace, not by obeying rules about foods, which do not help those who obey them.

HEBREWS 13:9 NCV

Don't fret or worry. Instead of worrying, pray. Let petitions and praises shape your worries into prayers, letting God know your concerns. Before you know it, a sense of God's wholeness, everything coming together for good, will come and settle you down. It's wonderful what happens when Christ displaces worry at the center of your life.

PHILIPPIANS 4:6–7 MSG

I will confess and praise You for You are fearful and wonderful and for the awful wonder of my birth! Wonderful are Your works, and that my inner self knows right well.

PSALM 139:14 AMP

In the multitude of my [anxious] thoughts within me, Your comforts cheer and delight my soul!

PSALM 94:19 AMP

"Therefore I tell you, do not worry about your life, what you will eat or drink; or about your body, what you will wear. Is not life more than food, and the body more than clothes? Look at the birds of the air; they do not sow or reap or store away in barns, and yet your heavenly Father feeds them. Are you not much more valuable than they? Can any one of you by worrying add a single hour to your life? And why do you worry about clothes? See how the flowers of the field grow. They do not labor or spin. Yet I tell you that not even Solomon in all his splendor was dressed like one of these. If that is how God clothes the grass of the field, which is here today and tomorrow is thrown into the fire, will he not much more clothe you—you of little faith? So do not worry, saying, 'What shall we eat?' or 'What shall we drink?' or 'What shall we wear?' For the pagans run after all these things, and your heavenly Father knows that you need them. But seek first his kingdom and his righteousness, and all these things will be given to you as well. Therefore do not worry about tomorrow, for tomorrow will worry about itself. Each day has enough trouble of its own."

MATTHEW 6:25–34 NIV

But the wisdom from above is first of all pure. It is also peace loving, gentle at all times, and willing to yield to others. It is full of mercy and good deeds. It shows no favoritism and is always sincere.

JAMES 3:17 NLT

He has shown you, O mortal, what is good. And what does the LORD require of you? To act justly and to love mercy and to walk humbly with your God.

MICAH 6:8 NIV

For the Lord takes pleasure in His people; He will beautify the humble with salvation and adorn the wretched with victory.

PSALM 149:4 AMP

Let not mercy and kindness [shutting out all hatred and selfishness] and truth [shutting out all deliberate hypocrisy or falsehood] forsake you; bind them about your neck, write them upon the tablet of your heart. So shall you find favor, good understanding, and high esteem in the sight [or judgment] of God and man.

PROVERBS 3:3–4 AMP

Be beautiful in your heart by being gentle and quiet. This kind of beauty will last, and God considers it very special.

1 PETER 3:4 CEV

God
Understands
Me

Lord, I feel like no one understands me. How could anyone else know what I am going through? Even when my closest friends don't seem to "get me," I trust that You do, Father. You know every thought and desire that crosses my mind. Help me to have complete faith that You are always there and can understand me in a way that no one else in the world can. Amen.

The heart is deceitful above all things and beyond cure. Who can understand it? "I the LORD search the heart and examine the mind, to reward each person according to their conduct, according to what their deeds deserve."

JEREMIAH 17:9–10 NIV

In certain ways we are weak, but the Spirit is here to help us. For example, when we don't know what to pray for, the Spirit prays for us in ways that cannot be put into words.

ROMANS 8:26 CEV

"And be sure of this: I am with you always, even to the end of the age."

MATTHEW 28:20 NLT

If any of you lacks wisdom, you should ask God, who gives generously to all without finding fault, and it will be given to you. But when you ask, you must believe and not doubt, because the one who doubts is like a wave of the sea, blown and tossed by the wind. That person should not expect to receive anything from the Lord. Such a person is double-minded and unstable in all they do.

JAMES 1:5–8 NIV

Joyful is the person who finds wisdom, the one who gains understanding. For wisdom is more profitable than silver, and her wages are better than gold. Wisdom is more precious than rubies; nothing you desire can compare with her.

PROVERBS 3:13–15 NLT

You, LORD, hear the desire of the afflicted; you encourage them, and you listen to their cry, defending the fatherless and the oppressed, so that mere earthly mortals will never again strike terror.

PSALM 10:17–18 NIV

For thus says the High and Lofty One who inhabits eternity, whose name is Holy: "I dwell in the high and holy place, with him who has a contrite and humble spirit, to revive the spirit of the humble, and to revive the heart of the contrite ones."

ISAIAH 57:15 NKJV

So turn to God! Give up your sins, and you will be forgiven. Then that time will come when the Lord will give you fresh strength. He will send you Jesus, his chosen Messiah.

ACTS 3:19–20 CEV

The LORD is a shelter for the oppressed, a refuge in times of trouble. Those who know your name trust in you, for you, O LORD, do not abandon those who search for you.

PSALM 9:9–10 NLT

"Well, there they are—your servants, your people whom you so powerfully and impressively redeemed. O Master, listen to me, listen to your servant's prayer—and yes, to all your servants who delight in honoring you—and make me successful today so that I get what I want from the king."

NEHEMIAH 1:11 MSG

"For the mountains shall depart and the hills be removed, but My kindness shall not depart from you, nor shall My covenant of peace be removed," says the LORD, who has mercy on you.

ISAIAH 54:10 NKJV

"I am leaving you with a gift—peace of mind and heart. And the peace I give is a gift the world cannot give. So don't be troubled or afraid."

JOHN 14:27 NLT

But the LORD said to Samuel, "Don't judge by his appearance or height, for I have rejected him. The LORD doesn't see things the way you see them. People judge by outward appearance, but the LORD looks at the heart."

1 SAMUEL 16:7 NLT

"Accept the God of your father. Serve him completely and willingly, because the LORD knows what is in everyone's mind. He understands everything you think. If you go to him for help, you will get an answer."

1 CHRONICLES 28:9 NCV

All praise to the God and Father of our Master, Jesus the Messiah! Father of all mercy! God of all healing counsel! He comes alongside us when we go through hard times, and before you know it, he brings us alongside someone else who is going through hard times so that we can be there for that person just as God was there for us. We have plenty of hard times that come from following the Messiah, but no more so than the good times of his healing comfort—we get a full measure of that, too.

2 CORINTHIANS 1:3–5 MSG

So the LORD must wait for you to come to him so he can show you his love and compassion. For the LORD is a faithful God. Blessed are those who wait for his help.

ISAIAH 30:18 NLT

Consider it a sheer gift, friends, when tests and challenges come at you from all sides. You know that under pressure, your faith-life is forced into the open and shows its true colors. So don't try to get out of anything prematurely. Let it do its work so you become mature and well-developed, not deficient in any way.

JAMES 1:2–4 MSG

"These things I have spoken to you, that in Me you may have peace. In the world you will have tribulation; but be of good cheer, I have overcome the world."

JOHN 16:33 NKJV

The fear of the LORD is the beginning of wisdom: and the knowledge of the holy is understanding.

PROVERBS 9:10 KJV

If you need wisdom, ask our generous God, and he will give it to you. He will not rebuke you for asking.

JAMES 1:5 NLT

But now, GOD's Message, the God who made you in the first place, Jacob, the One who got you started, Israel: "Don't be afraid, I've redeemed you. I've called your name. You're mine. When you're in over your head, I'll be there with you. When you're in rough waters, you will not go down. When you're between a rock and a hard place, it won't be a dead end—because I am GOD, your personal God, The Holy of Israel, your Savior. I paid a huge price for you. . . . That's how much you mean to me! That's how much I love you! I'd sell off the whole world to get you back, trade the creation just for you."

ISAIAH 43:2 MSG

What we have received is not the spirit of the world, but the Spirit who is from God, so that we may understand what God has freely given us. This is what we speak, not in words taught us by human wisdom but in words taught by the Spirit, explaining spiritual realities with Spirit-taught words.

1 CORINTHIANS 2:12–13 NIV

The Lord bless you and watch, guard, and keep you; the Lord make His face to shine upon and enlighten you and be gracious (kind, merciful, and giving favor) to you; the Lord lift up His [approving] countenance upon you and give you peace (tranquility of heart and life continually).

NUMBERS 6:24–26 AMP

Search me [thoroughly], O God, and know my heart! Try me and know my thoughts! And see if there is any wicked or hurtful way in me, and lead me in the way everlasting.

PSALM 139:23–24 AMP

You are always making yourselves look good, but God sees what is in your heart. The things that most people think are important are worthless as far as God is concerned.

LUKE 16:15 CEV

God Wants
Me to Do the
Right Thing

Dear God, I know that You have a plan for my life and desire for me to do Your will—but I am often selfish and stubborn, wanting to please only myself. Help me to honor You in each choice I make. Give me strength and courage to always do the right thing. May it be obvious to everyone who knows me that there is something different about the way I act and the choices I make, because of my relationship with You. Amen.

Jesus replied: " 'Love the Lord your God with all your heart and with all your soul and with all your mind.' This is the first and greatest commandment. And the second is like it: 'Love your neighbor as yourself.' All the Law and the Prophets hang on these two commandments."

MATTHEW 22:37–40 NIV

If anyone boasts, "I love God," and goes right on hating his brother or sister, thinking nothing of it, he is a liar. If he won't love the person he can see, how can he love the God he can't see? The command we have from Christ is blunt: Loving God includes loving people. You've got to love both.

1 JOHN 4:20–21 MSG

For everything comes from him and exists by his power and is intended for his glory. All glory to him forever! Amen.

ROMANS 11:36 NLT

The sacrifice that honors me is a thankful heart. Obey me, and I, your God, will show my power to save.

PSALM 50:23 CEV

"If you remain in me and my words remain in you, ask whatever you wish, and it will be done for you. This is to my Father's glory, that you bear much fruit, showing yourselves to be my disciples."

JOHN 15:7–8 NIV

Let your light so shine before men, that they may see your good works, and glorify your Father which is in heaven.

MATTHEW 5:16 KJV

Not unto us, O LORD, not unto us, but to Your name give glory, because of Your mercy, because of Your truth.

PSALM 115:1 NKJV

Tell everyone of every nation, "Praise the glorious power of the LORD. He is wonderful! Praise him and bring an offering into his temple. Worship the LORD, majestic and holy."

1 CHRONICLES 16:28–29 CEV

People enjoy giving good advice. Saying the right word at the right time is so pleasing.

PROVERBS 15:23 NCV

Therefore, as God's chosen people, holy and dearly loved, clothe yourselves with compassion, kindness, humility, gentleness and patience. Bear with each other and forgive one another if any of you has a grievance against someone. Forgive as the Lord forgave you. And over all these virtues put on love, which binds them all together in perfect unity. Let the peace of Christ rule in your hearts, since as members of one body you were called to peace. And be thankful.

COLOSSIANS 3:12–15 NIV

But as for you, O man of God, flee from all these things; aim at and pursue righteousness (right standing with God and true goodness), godliness (which is the loving fear of God and being Christlike), faith, love, steadfastness (patience), and gentleness of heart.

1 TIMOTHY 6:11 AMP

May God give you more and more grace and peace as you grow in your knowledge of God and Jesus our Lord. By his divine power, God has given us everything we need for living a godly life. We have received all of this by coming to know him, the one who called us to himself by means of his marvelous glory and excellence.

2 PETER 1:2–3 NLT

My brothers and sisters, I am sure that you are full of goodness. I know that you have all the knowledge you need and that you are able to teach each other.

ROMANS 15:14 NCV

Consider it a sheer gift, friends, when tests and challenges come at you from all sides. You know that under pressure, your faith-life is forced into the open and shows its true colors. So don't try to get out of anything prematurely. Let it do its work so you become mature and well-developed, not deficient in any way.

JAMES 1:2–4 MSG

"You're blessed when you're at the end of your rope. With less of you there is more of God and his rule. You're blessed when you feel you've lost what is most dear to you. Only then can you be embraced by the One most dear to you. You're blessed when you're content with just who you are—no more, no less. That's the moment you find yourselves proud owners of everything that can't be bought. You're blessed when you've worked up a good appetite for God. He's food and drink in the best meal you'll ever eat. You're blessed when you care. At the moment of being 'care-full,' you find yourselves cared for. You're blessed when you get your inside world—your mind and heart—put right. Then you can see God in the outside world. You're blessed when you can show people how to cooperate instead of compete or fight. That's when you discover who you really are, and your place in God's family. You're blessed when your commitment to God provokes persecution. The persecution drives you even deeper into God's kingdom."

MATTHEW 5:3–10 MSG

Do not repay evil with evil or insult with insult. On the contrary, repay evil with blessing, because to this you were called so that you may inherit a blessing.

1 PETER 3:9 NIV

"The person who knows my commandments and keeps them, that's who loves me. And the person who loves me will be loved by my Father, and I will love him and make myself plain to him."

JOHN 14:21 MSG

The Spirit Himself [thus] testifies together with our own spirit, [assuring us] that we are children of God. And if we are [His] children, then we are [His] heirs also: heirs of God and fellow heirs with Christ [sharing His inheritance with Him]; only we must share His suffering if we are to share His glory.

ROMANS 8:16–17 AMP

"But love your enemies, do good to them, and lend to them without expecting to get anything back. Then your reward will be great, and you will be children of the Most High, because he is kind to the ungrateful and wicked."

LUKE 6:35 NIV

You belong to the light and live in the day. We don't live in the night or belong to the dark.

1 THESSALONIANS 5:5 CEV

Watch your words and hold your tongue; you'll save yourself a lot of grief.

PROVERBS 21:23 MSG

This is how we know what real love is: Jesus gave his life for us. So we should give our lives for our brothers and sisters.

1 JOHN 3:16 NCV

You were bought with a price [purchased with a preciousness and paid for, made His own]. So then, honor God and bring glory to Him in your body.

1 CORINTHIANS 6:20 AMP

Stop being angry and don't try to take revenge. I am the LORD, and I command you to love others as much as you love yourself.

LEVITICUS 19:18 CEV

And God's servants must not be troublemakers. They must be kind to everyone, and they must be good teachers and very patient. Be humble when you correct people who oppose you. Maybe God will lead them to turn to him and learn the truth.

2 TIMOTHY 2:24–25 CEV

Create in me a pure heart, God, and make my spirit right again.

PSALM 51:10 NCV

But the Holy Spirit produces this kind of fruit in our lives: love, joy, peace, patience, kindness, goodness, faithfulness, gentleness, and self-control. There is no law against these things!

GALATIANS 5:22–23 NLT

And be not conformed to this world: but be ye transformed by the renewing of your mind, that ye may prove what is that good, and acceptable, and perfect, will of God.

ROMANS 12:2 KJV

Rather, as servants of God we commend ourselves in every way: in great endurance; in troubles, hardships and distresses; in beatings, imprisonments and riots; in hard work, sleepless nights and hunger; in purity, understanding, patience and kindness; in the Holy Spirit and in sincere love; in truthful speech and in the power of God; with weapons of righteousness in the right hand and in the left; through glory and dishonor, bad report and good report; genuine, yet regarded as impostors; known, yet regarded as unknown; dying, and yet we live on; beaten, and yet not killed; sorrowful, yet always rejoicing; poor, yet making many rich; having nothing, and yet possessing everything.

2 CORINTHIANS 6:4–10 NIV

The answer is, if you eat or drink, or if you do anything, do it all for the glory of God.

1 CORINTHIANS 10:31 NCV

And you must love the LORD your God with all your heart, all your soul, and all your strength.

DEUTERONOMY 6:5 NLT

So once again, I, the LORD All-Powerful, tell you, "See that justice is done and be kind and merciful to one another! Don't mistreat widows or orphans or foreigners or anyone who is poor, and stop making plans to hurt each other."

ZECHARIAH 7:9–10 CEV

But as the One Who called you is holy, you yourselves also be holy in all your conduct and manner of living. For it is written, You shall be holy, for I am holy.

1 PETER 1:15–16 AMP

Don't let anyone make fun of you, just because you are young. Set an example for other followers by what you say and do, as well as by your love, faith, and purity.

1 TIMOTHY 4:12 CEV

Therefore, since we have these promises, dear friends, let us purify ourselves from everything that contaminates body and spirit, perfecting holiness out of reverence for God.

2 CORINTHIANS 7:1 NIV

God Wants Me to Read His Word

Father, You gave us the Bible as a way to know You better and as a reminder of all the things You have done because You love us so much. To grow closer to You, I need to read Your Word and allow it to influence my life. Help me to have the discipline to make Bible reading an everyday part of my life. Open my heart so I may be encouraged and inspired by each verse that I read. Thank You for the truth of Your Word, Lord. Amen.

I have taken your words to heart so I would not sin
against you.

PSALM 119:11 NCV

I have written to you who are God's children because
you know the Father. I have written to you who are
mature in the faith because you know Christ, who
existed from the beginning. I have written to you
who are young in the faith because you are strong.
God's word lives in your hearts, and you have won
your battle with the evil one.

1 JOHN 2:14 NLT

Pay attention to advice and accept correction, so you
can live sensibly.

PROVERBS 19:20 CEV

"But all this was done that the Scriptures of the
prophets might be fulfilled."

MATTHEW 26:56 NKJV

Everything God says is true—and it's a shield for all
who come to him for safety.

PROVERBS 30:5 CEV

"It is the same with my word. I send it out, and it always produces fruit. It will accomplish all I want it to, and it will prosper everywhere I send it."

ISAIAH 55:11 NLT

The Spirit of Christ was in them and was telling them how Christ would suffer and would then be given great honor. So they searched to find out exactly who Christ would be and when this would happen. But they were told that they were serving you and not themselves. They preached to you by the power of the Holy Spirit, who was sent from heaven. And their message was only for you, even though angels would like to know more about it.

1 PETER 1:11–12 CEV

The Word was first, the Word present to God, God present to the Word. The Word was God, in readiness for God from day one.

JOHN 1:1–2 MSG

For whatever was thus written in former days was written for our instruction, that by [our steadfast and patient] endurance and the encouragement [drawn] from the Scriptures we might hold fast to and cherish hope.

ROMANS 15:4 AMP

Jesus answered, "You don't understand, because you don't know what the Scriptures say, and you don't know about the power of God."

MATTHEW 22:29 NCV

Finally, be strong in the Lord and in his mighty power. Put on the full armor of God, so that you can take your stand against the devil's schemes. For our struggle is not against flesh and blood, but against the rulers, against the authorities, against the powers of this dark world and against the spiritual forces of evil in the heavenly realms. Therefore put on the full armor of God, so that when the day of evil comes, you may be able to stand your ground, and after you have done everything, to stand. Stand firm then, with the belt of truth buckled around your waist, with the breastplate of righteousness in place, and with your feet fitted with the readiness that comes from the gospel of peace. In addition to all this, take up the shield of faith, with which you can extinguish all the flaming arrows of the evil one. Take the helmet of salvation and the sword of the Spirit, which is the word of God.

EPHESIANS 6:10–17 NIV

LORD, your word is everlasting; it continues forever in heaven.

PSALM 119:89 NCV

I want you to recall the words spoken in the past by the holy prophets and the command given by our Lord and Savior through your apostles.

2 PETER 3:2 NIV

Long ago in many ways and at many times God's prophets spoke his message to our ancestors. But now at last, God sent his Son to bring his message to us. God created the universe by his Son, and everything will someday belong to the Son.

HEBREWS 1:1–2 CEV

Let the teaching of Christ live in you richly. Use all wisdom to teach and instruct each other by singing psalms, hymns, and spiritual songs with thankfulness in your hearts to God.

COLOSSIANS 3:16 NCV

Your word is a lamp for my feet, a light on my path.

PSALM 119:105 NIV

Most of all, you must understand this: No prophecy in the Scriptures ever comes from the prophet's own interpretation. No prophecy ever came from what a person wanted to say, but people led by the Holy Spirit spoke words from God.

2 PETER 1:20–21 NCV

For the word of God is alive and powerful. It is sharper than the sharpest two-edged sword, cutting between soul and spirit, between joint and marrow. It exposes our innermost thoughts and desires.

HEBREWS 4:12 NLT

There's nothing like the written Word of God for showing you the way to salvation through faith in Christ Jesus. Every part of Scripture is God-breathed and useful one way or another—showing us truth, exposing our rebellion, correcting our mistakes, training us to live God's way. Through the Word we are put together and shaped up for the tasks God has for us.

2 TIMOTHY 3:15–17 MSG

Like newborn babies you should crave (thirst for, earnestly desire) the pure (unadulterated) spiritual milk, that by it you may be nurtured and grow unto [completed] salvation.

1 PETER 2:2 AMP

Therefore you shall lay up these My words in your [minds and] hearts and in your [entire] being, and bind them for a sign upon your hands and as forehead bands between your eyes. And you shall teach them to your children, speaking of them when you sit in your house and when you walk along the road, when you lie down and when you rise up.

DEUTERONOMY 11:18–19 AMP

Seek the LORD while He may be found, call upon Him while He is near.

ISAIAH 55:6 NKJV

The one thing I ask of the LORD—the thing I seek most—is to live in the house of the LORD all the days of my life, delighting in the LORD's perfections and meditating in his Temple.

PSALM 27:4 NLT

We know that the Law is spiritual. But I am merely a human, and I have been sold as a slave to sin. In fact, I don't understand why I act the way I do. I don't do what I know is right. I do the things I hate. Although I don't do what I know is right, I agree that the Law is good. So I am not the one doing these evil things. The sin that lives in me is what does them. I know that my selfish desires won't let me do anything that is good. Even when I want to do right, I cannot. Instead of doing what I know is right, I do wrong.

ROMANS 7:14–19 CEV

My heart has heard you say, "Come and talk with me." And my heart responds, "LORD, I am coming."

PSALM 27:8 NLT

This Book of the Law shall not depart out of your mouth, but you shall meditate on it day and night, that you may observe and do according to all that is written in it. For then you shall make your way prosperous, and then you shall deal wisely and have good success.

JOSHUA 1:8 AMP

Blessed (happy, fortunate, prosperous, and enviable) is the man who walks and lives not in the counsel of the ungodly [following their advice, their plans and purposes], nor stands [submissive and inactive] in the path where sinners walk, nor sits down [to relax and rest] where the scornful [and the mockers] gather. But his delight and desire are in the law of the Lord, and on His law (the precepts, the instructions, the teachings of God) he habitually meditates (ponders and studies) by day and by night. And he shall be like a tree firmly planted [and tended] by the streams of water, ready to bring forth its fruit in its season; its leaf also shall not fade or wither; and everything he does shall prosper [and come to maturity].

PSALM 1:1–3 AMP

There are different kinds of spiritual gifts, but they all come from the same Spirit. There are different ways to serve the same Lord.

1 CORINTHIANS 12:4–5 CEV

Who, then, are those who fear the LORD? He will instruct them in the ways they should choose. They will spend their days in prosperity, and their descendants will inherit the land. The LORD confides in those who fear him; he makes his covenant known to them.

PSALM 25:12–14 NIV

And so, dear brothers and sisters, I plead with you to give your bodies to God because of all he has done for you. Let them be a living and holy sacrifice—the kind he will find acceptable. This is truly the way to worship him. Don't copy the behavior and customs of this world, but let God transform you into a new person by changing the way you think. Then you will learn to know God's will for you, which is good and pleasing and perfect.

ROMANS 12:1–2 NLT

Pray also for me, that whenever I speak, words may be given me so that I will fearlessly make known the mystery of the gospel, for which I am an ambassador in chains. Pray that I may declare it fearlessly, as I should.

EPHESIANS 6:19–20 NIV

In God (I will praise His word), in God I have put my trust; I will not fear.

PSALM 56:4 NKJV

Look for these other God ♥s Me products...

God ♥s Me:
A Devotional Journal for Girls

God ♥s Me:
New Life™ Version Bible for Girls

Available wherever Christian books are sold.